London's
Great Railway
Century
1850–1950

D0892519

LONDON'S
GREAT RAILWAY
CENTURY
1850–1950

KEITH SCHOLEY

This book is dedicated to my good friend
and comrade Jonathan Cohen

First published 2012

The History Press
The Mill, Brimscombe Port
Stroud, Gloucestershire, GL5 2QG
www.thehistorypress.co.uk

British Library Cataloguing in Publication Data.
A catalogue record for this book is available from the British Library.

ISBN 978 0 7524 6291 2

Typesetting and origination by The History Press
Printed in Great Britain

Contents

Introduction

The hundred years from 1850 to 1950 were the Railway Century, the great era during which the railway was the supreme method of transportation. London was the railway capital of the world: the city with the most developed railway network on the planet, where ancient railway relics sat side by side with innovative technology and the gritty work of the goods station contrasted with the plush splendour of the railway hotels. Railways were the capital's arteries, trains the lifeblood.

During the early years, each railway line was self-contained, complete in itself, with individual quirkiness in gauge or motive power a mere incidental. However, the burgeoning economy required an interconnected network and the whims and oddities of the early lines were soon abolished (*see* 1850: Whims and Oddities: Eccentricities of London's Early Railways).

Within a ten-year period, the new method of transport was well established as the way to travel long distance. To cope with the new traffic, the original makeshift buildings of the termini were replaced by a new breed of giants. Huge arched roofs fronted by classical-style blocks made the railway station an immediately recognisable form of architecture (*see* 1860: At the Railway Station: London's Early Termini).

The next decade saw the railway blossom as intra-urban transport. The spaces between the main lines were filled with a spider's web of branches and loops, and, as a result, the City of London emptied and suburban villas filled with what we would know as commuters. The great boom was particularly felt in the south (*see* 1870: Tomorrow to Fresh Woods, and Pastures New: South London Suburban Boom).

A rather slower growth was experienced by the first underground railways – the Metropolitan and District. Opened in 1863, the Metropolitan was the first underground railway in the world, matching technological innovation with competent engineering. A particular feature of these lines was the circular services (*see* 1880: About, About, in Reel and Rout: London's Railway Circles).

The magnificent hotels attached to most of the main termini were prominent and unique features of London's railway life. These offered not just overnight accommodation but also splendid restaurants and noble meeting places. These had their heyday in the 'gay nineties' (*see* 1890: Now Night Comes On: London's Railway Hotels).

The backbone of the railway system, providing the old companies with more than half of their revenue, was the goods trade. Hidden from view but vital to the health and vitality of the capital were the great goods stations, where everything imaginable was loaded and unloaded, stored and delivered (*see* 1900: With Peacock's Eyes and the Wares of Carthage: London's Goods Depots).

The twentieth century saw radical new developments based on the miracle power of electricity. This was first applied underground. Surface development had become prohibitively expensive; the new technology meant that deep-level railways were now a practical proposition. Here, again, London was a world leader (*see* 1910: A Traveller Came By, Silently, Invisibly: London's First Tubes).

Existing railways also got the electric treatment. This was applied mainly to suburban routes, of which London already had an ample supply. In the early years, until 1920 or so, Britain was the leading nation in Europe, if not the world, so far as railway electrification was concerned (*see* 1920: Early Electric! London's Suburban Electrics).

The interwar years were a period of stagnation for Britain as a whole and for its railways in particular. Despite this there were a number of interesting developments, for instance in relation to the private railways serving the capital's various services, which were at their height of diversity at this time (*see* 1930: The Light and the Water, Earth and Men – London's Industrial Railways.

The Second World War saw the start of the irreversible decline of the old railway world. It was also their finest hour when, despite bomb and bullet, the railways 'carried on'. Nowhere was the devastation more prominently displayed than in the City of London, which received more than its fair share of fire from above (*see* 1940: The Injustice of the Skies: The City's Railways Blitzed).

Post-war, London's railways, like Britain itself, were in a sorry state, desperately in need of the reinvestment that only the state could apparently provide. However, their time had passed. In future, the railways would have a secondary role as auxiliaries to road transport and for commuters. Increasingly marginalised, what was life became 'interest', the niche of the 'spotter' (*see* 1950: Base Details London's Engine Sheds).

The course of events in London was mirrored in Britain as a whole. What held good for Britain, however, did not hold good for the world. Most other countries have a more positive attitude to rail transport, both historically and at present. The ongoing second railway age may prove to be a turnaround. Despite this, the great railway century has left a lasting legacy.

Eccentricities of London's Early Railways

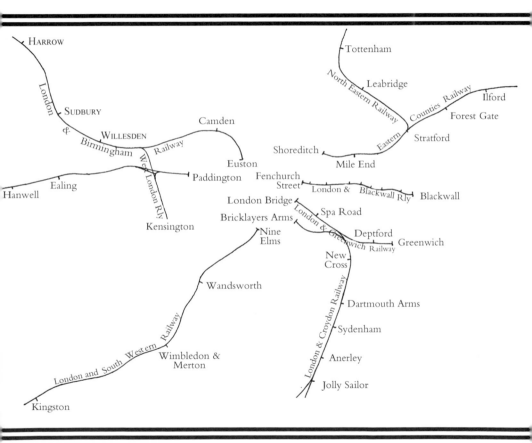

Eccentricities of London's railways before 1850.

The railway era in London began with the opening of the first suburban line (London and Greenwich) in 1836 and the first main line (London and Birmingham) the following year. A rash of lines followed over the next decade. The most interesting of these early railways were those with non-standard features:

Right-hand running   London and Greenwich Railway

Bi-directional running   London and Blackwall Railway

Left-hand running on the railways was adopted following the custom on the roads. There was no special reason for this because the railways were entirely independent of the existing road transport system. Left-hand running was hence arbitrary but not unanimous, the few exceptions due to special circumstances.

Broad gauge   Eastern Counties Railway (5ft)
                                Northern and Eastern Railway (5ft)
                                London and Blackwall Railway (5ft)
                                Great Western Railway (7ft ¼in)

Gauge: in short the broader the better. The broader the gauge, the lower the centre of gravity of the rolling stock and the more stable the trains, especially over curves at speed. In Britain, however, most railways, influenced by Stephenson's familiarity with the operation of 4ft 8½in in the long-established tramways of the north-east, adopted the current, relatively narrow, gauge – now known as Standard. A higher rate of railway accidents has been the price paid for the poor choice made in the early Victorian era. Interestingly, elsewhere a broader gauge was victorious (see Annexe: Broad and Narrow).

Rope haulage   London and Blackwall Railway
                                London and Birmingham Railway (Euston to
                                   Camden)
                                London and South Western Railway (Nine Elms)

Atmospheric haulage   London and Croydon Railway (New Cross to
                                   Croydon)

Traction: Steam was always recognised as unsatisfactory. As well as being noisy and dirty, it was also inefficient both in terms of manpower and energy usage. However, as the failures of cable haulage and pneumatic experiments in the pre-1850 era showed, there was no alternative. In the 1860s pneumatic systems were again investigated. During the late Victorian era, electric traction became a practical alternative. However, the large initial costs hindered development and the demise of steam came only after the introduction of the cheap functional diesel-electric motor.

The early railways could possess such eccentricities because it was assumed that each line would be self-contained. However, the costs involved in construction meant that traffic-generating connections were vital. By 1850 most oddities had been removed, creating an interconnected network between London and the rest of the country.

London and Greenwich Railway

Right-hand running was the minor, albeit rare, eccentricity of the London and Greenwich (L&G) and was a short-term arrangement to cope with operating difficulties.

At the time of the line's opening in February 1836, only the central section from Deptford to Spa Road was finished. The terminal stations at London Bridge and Greenwich with space for shunting were unavailable. A system known as 'fly-shunting' was used to cope with this. This had the benefit of enabling a

Transhipment of goods, *c*.1850: differing gauges and methods of motive power brought chaos to the rails. (*Illustrated London News*)

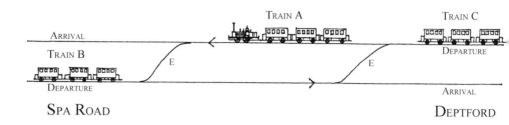

Fly-shunting, London & Greenwich Railway.

single engine to work three trains consecutively. The system of working was quite simple but is best illustrated by reference to the diagram above. Just before reaching the points near Spa Road the guard on the first carriage on Train A 'casts off' his engine on a signal from the driver and the guards apply the brake on the carriages. The engine runs through the facing points to the departure platform at Spa Road towards Train B. The points are then changed so that the carriages can run to a stop at the arrival platform at Spa Road. Train B is then coupled to and led out by the engine (running backwards). The procedure is repeated at Deptford for Train C. It is not known how the carriages were transferred from departure to arrival platforms but horses could have been used. The London & Greenwich had intended to run on the left and as was the custom had installed trailing points at intervals along the line. Fly-shunting required facing points. It was a simple matter to reverse the up and down lines as there was no intention of through running.

Right-hand running continued until April 1839. This was some time after completion of the line – possibly once established, the practice became a habit hard to break. It might have continued longer had the isolation of the line not been broken by the intrusion in June of the London and Croydon which connected up to the Greenwich line at Corbett's Lane Junction.

This is not the end of the story, however. In 1850, the viaduct between Corbett's Lane and London Bridge was widened and its tracks rearranged. The South Eastern, the new owners of the London and Greenwich, decided to again reverse the order of the Greenwich tracks to give the best arrangement for speeding traffic and avoiding fouling lines. Despite schemes to abolish this, it continued until May 1901, when the viaduct was once again widened. The Greenwich line was finally normalised.

London and South Western Railway

The eccentricity of the London and South Western Railway (LSWR) was also relatively minor. At the Nine Elms terminus from its opening in 1838 until 1848, when the line was extended to Waterloo, trains ran into and out of the station without locomotives.

Running in was easy – generally by momentum. Coming out, horses may have been used. This was little bother as the lightweight four-wheeler carriages of the day were easily manoeuvred. Moving empty stock about using horse power was then widespread; however to ban engines from entering a passenger station was unusual (although universal at goods stations). At Nine Elms it was a sensible practice as the platforms and train shed were wooden and hence highly flammable. The procedure was time-consuming however, and although also used at London Bridge and Waterloo, was not to be found after about 1860.

London and Birmingham Railway

Between 1836 and 1844 the London and Birmingham (L&B) had a short section (around 1 mile) of rope haulage from its terminus at Euston to the locomotive depot at Camden.

Nine Elms station, c.1838: the fine classical building by architectural maestro William Tite hid an inflammable wooden shed. (From an old print)

The problem was ostensibly a technical one. The ascent, known as Camden Bank, had a severe gradient and the company's engineer, the famous Robert Stephenson, reputedly doubted the ability of contemporary engines to cope with the bank. However, rope haulage could also have been used to placate objections to the dirty and noisy intrusion of the railway into the area of high-class housing. Carriages were attached to an 'endless rope' and then hauled up by stationary engines in a chamber below the line. Trains ran down to Euston by gravity with braking by rule of thumb. All employees were trained in this art and top brass would sometimes do the honours: '…when the first Napoleon's celebrated general, Marshal Soult, paid us the honour of a visit, I assisted the General Manager and the Superintendent of Police in lowering the train to Euston, ordinary brakesmen being put aside on so important an occasion.' (David Stevenson, *Fifty Years on the London and North Western Railway*, 1891)

The problem of compatibility was not a problem. Technologically, however, the setup was unnecessary (for the first few months trains were double-headed instead) and worked unsatisfactorily (the 'skid' at the rear of the trains would come loose and thrash about like a wild creature or the leader rope would break). The primitive signal apparatus, which consisted of coloured water in a tube and a whistle, also failed occasionally. The practice of stopping trains by braking was obviously a potential danger due to out-of-control trains. Moreover, it was time-consuming.

The arrangement was dispensed with in 1844 and was replaced with the practice of double-heading, which lasted throughout most of the steam era. The

Euston station, 1838: here are the carriages – no locomotives allowed. (Author's collection)

winding engines were removed and sold on for further use and the chimneys were demolished. The engine chambers below the line remain today however, echoing hulks of a bygone era.

Eastern Counties and Northern and Eastern Railways

For a brief time broad gauge looked certain to rule east of London as well as to the west, however the lines involved acted unusually efficiently and standardised early.

It was originally planned to carry out the Eastern Counties – London's connection with East Anglia – in the Great Western's 7ft ¼in gauge. However, cost considerations soon narrowed the line and the first section opened in June 1839 in 5ft gauge. The Northern and Eastern (N&E) on the other hand was originally viewed as a standard-gauge line to Cambridge. Impoverishment meant it dropped the idea of a separate terminus, joining up instead with the Eastern Counties at Stratford. The N&E was thus forced to adopt the 5ft gauge – doubtless much to the chagrin of Robert Stephenson, the N&E's engineer and the most vehement advocate of 4ft 8½in. The N&E was opened as far as Broxbourne in the autumn of 1840.

At first little importance was attached to the gauge question; however, with an eye to future developments, both lines were standardised in October 1844.

Lea Bridge station, c.1890: this was one of the few lasting relics of the old N&E – reduction of gauge made little difference to the space between the tracks. (Author's collection)

Great Western Railway

The Great Western Railway's (GWR) broad gauge was the most enduring of the major eccentricities. But although it survived long after 1850, it was already effectively doomed.

As is well known, the GWR adopted the 7ft gauge on the advice of the legendary Isambard Kingdom Brunel. The decision had a good technical basis but, by the time the GWR was completed through to Bristol in 1841, 4ft 8½in was already established as the national standard. At first the difference was not important but soon problems were identified and a Royal Commission was duly appointed.

The Gauge Commission made its report in July 1846. First, it compared the working of broad and 'narrow' gauge. Broad proved safer, passengers had a smoother ride, and, although initial outlay was slightly greater, running costs were the same. Indeed the only real advantage of standard was the greater manoeuvrability of its smaller goods wagons. However, the commission came down against broad gauge, recommending that all new lines be standard and that all broad-gauge lines be converted. One reason given was that the difficulties of interchange slowed traffic and held back economic development. However military planning was also important; a change of gauge involved detraining troops and slowed deployment. A uniform gauge was, therefore, considered desirable: 4ft 8½in was to be adopted because of its greater existing extent. In the event, no action was taken because of the belief in 'leaving commercial enterprise unfettered' but the principle was clearly established.

Paddington station, 1838: primitive conditions on the early broad gauge – was this always intended to be a temporary arrangement? (Author's collection)

In the London area in 1850, the broad gauge was almost entirely limited to the GWR main line. It was true that the goods-only West London Railway was fitted out with mixed gauge rails (with an additional outer rail for wide-gauge stock); however, broad-gauge engines did not run on the line at this time, broad-gauge wagons being hauled by standard-gauge locomotives, sometimes in dangerous mixed-gauge trains.

The five years after 1859 saw a great expansion of the broad gauge. In that year the Great Western reached the river with a single-track line to Brentford. Four years later broad-gauge trains began to run to Victoria via the West London railways and to Farringdon Street on the Metropolitan. The year 1864 saw the broad gauge at its maximum extent after the opening of the Hammersmith and City (H&C).

The downfall of broad gauge was undoubtedly due to the difficulties raised by incompatibility. These were particularly highlighted during the introduction of through-running suburban services in the 1860s that were not economical by the mixed-gauge method. Broad-gauge passenger services thus came off the West London in 1866, the H&C in 1868 and the Metropolitan in 1869. Already, in 1861, standard-gauge services had commenced on the main line and the Brentford branch (unusually on the latter a separate standard-gauge track was laid alongside the existing broad gauge). The desirability of through running of goods wagons meant that goods services were next and by the 1870s broad-gauge goods trains were an endangered species. The last preserve was the fast passenger expresses on the main line, which were the most advantageous use of the wider gauge. The final broad-gauge train ran on 20 May 1892. Because of the noticeably wider viaducts and bridges, occasional traces of the broad gauge may be visible even today.

London and Croydon Railway

Elsewhere, deviant forms of traction were temporary measures to deal with technical or environmental problems. In the case of the London and Croydon Railway (L&C) however, the introduction of atmospheric haulage was really more like a large-scale field trial.

The London and Croydon was a conventional railway when it opened in June 1839. Atmospheric haulage was approved, on the advice of Benjamin Cubitt, the company's engineer, in April 1844. This must have been largely on cost grounds since coal for the cash-strapped southern lines was expensive. Atmospheric traction promised big savings. Various systems had been previously tried out in Paris, Devon and Ireland, following a small-scale experiment at Wormwood Scrubs in West London.

The system adopted was that of Messrs Clegg and Samuda. A metal tube 15in in diameter was laid midway between the running rails. A slot ran along the top. This was covered by a leather flap, which was usually held down by metal plates and rods. A mix of beeswax and tallow made an airtight seal. The driving unit consisted of two 'carriages' (really something like wagons). Attached to the underside of the first 'carriage' was an iron plate which was made to pass under the side of the flap. The plate was attached to a piston inside the tube. Stationary engines at intervals along the line pumped the air out of the tube in front of the train, creating a vacuum and causing the piston to be sucked forward. On the second 'carriage' a 'heater' containing hot charcoal pressed against the wax and tallow to make the flap airtight again. Speeds of up to 70mph were claimed but 40–50mph was more realistic. Pumping stations were provided at Forest Hill, Norwood and Croydon. Like the passenger stations, the pump houses were carried out in the homely fashion sometimes called cottage orné and were similar to those on the Bedford to Bletchley line. The tall chimneys were disguised as ornate towers to please fussy residents. The running equipment was installed on a new track to the east of the existing two-track formation.

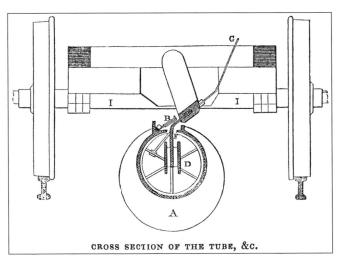

CROSS SECTION OF THE TUBE, &C.

Cross section of the tube, 1845: reference to the letters will show how the system worked. (*Illustrated London News*)

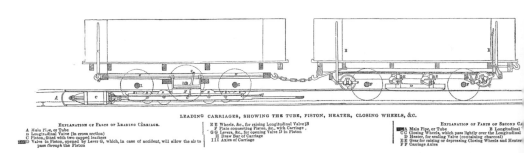

LEADING CARRIAGES, SHOWING THE TUBE, PISTON, HEATER, CLOSING WHEELS, &C.

Leading carriages, 1845: what, no loco? (*Illustrated London News*)

Test runs began in late 1845 with public service from Croydon to Forest Hill beginning on 19 January 1846. Early the following year an extension was made to New Cross (the nearest wholly owned L&C station to the centre). The most impressive technical feature was the flyover at Norwood. This was necessary to avoid crossing the Brighton main line on the level, and is claimed as the first of its type in the world. It was intended to continue the atmospheric track to London Bridge and Epsom; however, this did not come to pass.

West Croydon station, 1845: quaint, but what's this – the steeple is really a chimney! (*Illustrated London News*)

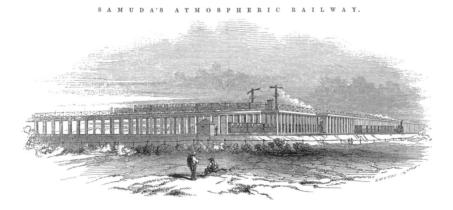

New Cross viaduct, 1845: a huge amount of building to avoid crossing an ordinary line on the level. (*Illustrated London News*)

The system failed largely on technical grounds. Although relatively efficient in fuel terms, maintenance was problematic – the trackside paraphernalia requiried constant repair. One particular problem was hungry rats, which took a fancy to the tasty leather flaps which were basted in beeswax and animal fat. It was, obviously, also not too compatible with the wider steam-powered system. And in June 1846 the London and Croydon ceased to be a local line when it amalgamated with the London and Brighton to form the London, Brighton and South Coast Railway. The new company viewed the abnormal haulage with jaundiced eyes and on 4 May 1847 the last atmospheric train was worked over the line. The apparatus was soon removed and the third track came into normal use. Relics, including tubes, are still occasionally unearthed to this day.

London and Blackwall Railway

The London and Blackwall (L&B), opened in July 1840, was undoubtedly the most deviational of the early railways in London. All other non-standard features derived from the choice of haulage, which was itself largely based on geographical considerations.

The London and Blackwall was originally envisaged as a completely ordinary railway. However the route ran through the densely packed slums of the East End and passed very close to the Regent's Canal Basin, where sailing vessels congregated. The fire risk was therefore very high. In addition it was considered that stopping and starting at the closely spaced halts would have taxed contemporary locomotives. The idea of using cable haulage to avoid these problems came from George Parker Bidder, once known as the 'Calculating Boy'. Cable or rope haulage was well established but was conventionally employed at sites with steep gradients (e.g. Camden). Having chosen a non-standard form of propulsion it was immaterial if a non-standard track width was selected and so a broad gauge was adopted as this promised greater stability at speed.

The actual method of working was unusual and interesting. At each end of the line were two large steam engines. These powered a drum which wound in a rope that ran in cast-iron sheaves between the running rails. The carriages had a platform at both ends. Here were located the levers for the brakes and the rope gripping equipment, which were operated by a guard or 'brakesman'. The standard train consisted of seven coaches, no locomotive being required. Starting from Minories or Blackwall, as the train passed along, one carriage was dropped at the rear and one carriage picked up at the front at each of the intermediate stations. Dropping was similar to the old slip coaches: the brakesman drew a pin from the coupling while the train was in motion, before braking to a halt. The main part of the train was therefore in continuous motion and a specific carriage was allocated to a specific station. Each of the two tracks was used alternately for up and down traffic to obviate the need for shunting.

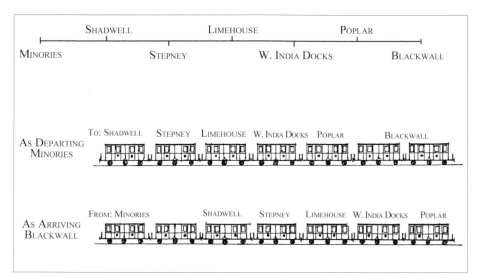

	SHADWELL		LIMEHOUSE		POPLAR	
MINORIES		STEPNEY		W. INDIA DOCKS		BLACKWALL

As Departing Minories

To: SHADWELL   STEPNEY   LIMEHOUSE   W. INDIA DOCKS   POPLAR   BLACKWALL

As Arriving Blackwall

FROM: MINORIES   SHADWELL   STEPNEY   LIMEHOUSE   W. INDIA DOCKS   POPLAR

Cable working, London & Blackwall Railway.

A station on the London & Blackwall Railway: the infrastructure of this line left much to be desired. (From an unidentified publication)

The system had its flaws – the most obvious was that there was no service from one intermediate station to another. The other was the tendency of the ropes to twist and snap. This was dangerous as the ropes would thrash about after breaking and replacement caused severe delays. A metal cable was substituted for the rope but the problem was only slightly ameliorated. Further to this, a goods service was difficult because of lack of flexibility.

Cable haulage was cheap, however, because of efficient fuel use; it was also safe, and gave a silent and smooth ride. Trains ran at 20–30mph – a reasonable speed for the day. The system was capable of some extension and in 1841 the line was built through to Fenchurch Street in the City. The short new stretch was ropeless, with trains running forward to the terminus under their own momentum and leaving by gravity.

Ultimately cable haulage was suited only to a self-enclosed urban passenger line (the Glasgow Subway used it for nearly thirty years). The cost of building the line required substantial returns which could only come from other railways. Connecting links were soon under construction to the Eastern Counties line and the North London. The last day of cable haulage was on 14 February 1849. The redundant apparatus was soon removed and the stationary winding engines sold on for further use. The engine chambers under the line were later in use as part of a goods depot and, although extensively altered, may survive today under the Docklands Light Railway station.

Annexe: Broad and Narrow

The British experience of the gauge question has been shared by most of Europe and North America. Early lines using non-standard widths were eventually converted, the smaller ones sooner rather than later. In the US, southern (5ft) and mid-western (4ft 10in) gauge held out for a while but had succumbed by late Victorian times. On the European periphery however, gauge irregularities have persisted.

In Portugal and Spain, Iberian gauge (5ft 5 in) is used. The width – a compromise between the old Portuguese gauge of 5ft 5½in (5 Portuguese feet) and the first Spanish gauge of 5ft 5⅚ in (6 Castilian feet) – was adopted early on (1845) and endured because of the isolation of the peninsula, both geographically (the Pyrenees) and politically (fascism during much of the twentieth century).

At the other end of the continent, Russian gauge – a cool 5ft, rejigged to 1,520mm everywhere except Finland – is used in the countries of the former Russian Empire. The width originated with American engineers who were employed by the Tsarists. The small difference gives no noticeable advantages but was retained partly to discourage invaders and partly due to the self-imposed isolation of the Communist period.

Ireland, oddly enough given that it was under the same political regime as mainland Britain for most of the railway age, also has a non-standard gauge – 5ft 3in. This was a British government decision based on the perceived advantages of the broader gauge but was close enough to standard to make

Kalka station, c.1900: Indians and a few Europeans swap generous broad for boxy narrow. (Author's collection)

conversion of locomotives easy. Irish gauge can also be found in a minor context in Brazil and Australia.

The widest gauge currently in use is the Indian gauge of 5ft 6in. Again, this was an imposition by the British government. As well as in India and its former territories of Bangladesh and Pakistan, the gauge is also in use in Argentina.

Gauges narrower than standard had little impact in Britain. Narrow has the advantage of cheaper construction costs and is operationally flexible, being better able to cope with tight curves, but is not suited to high-speed operation. The two main narrows currently in use are cape (3ft 6in) and metre (3ft 3⅜in) gauge. The former originated in Norway with the engineer Carl Phil but found favour in South Africa. It is the norm in developed countries such as Japan and New Zealand, as well as in more rugged environments including Southern and Central Africa and Queensland. Metre gauge dominates most of the rest of Africa, South America and South East Asia. Formerly the 3ft narrow gauge was widely used for feeders in Ireland and the US, with networks around Londonderry and Colorado respectively.

The most important multiple gauge countries are Argentina, Australia and India. In Argentina, Indian width dominates with a large metre-gauge network in the north and a speckle of standard-gauge lines. In Australia, conversion of Irish-gauge lines in Victoria to standard is ongoing but slow; the Queensland narrows are unlikely to be touched. Gauges really went wild in India: traditionally there were four: broad (5ft 6in), metre (3ft 3⅜in), narrow (2ft 6in) and tramway (2ft). All lines, excluding tourist hotspots, are being rapidly converted to broad as part of Project Unigauge.

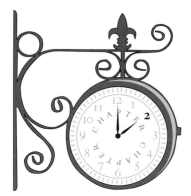

London's Early Termini

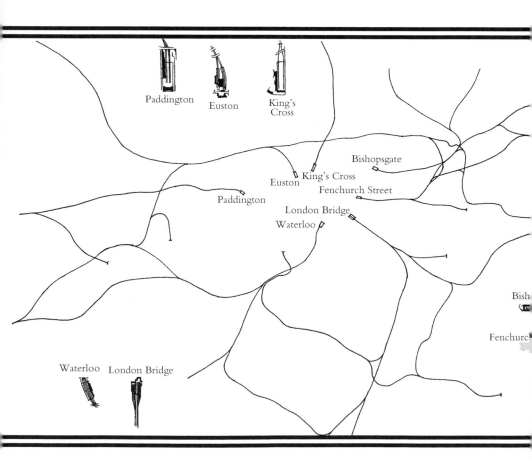

London's termini in 1860.

William Powell Frith's 'The Railway Station': a fine painting but now very unfashionable. (Author's collection)

Although in 1860 the railway terminus had been around for nearly a quarter of a century it was only at this point that it became an English institution. The event that marked this was the creation of William Powell Frith's painting 'The Railway Station'.

Frith began work in the autumn of 1860 and the picture was completed in March 1862. His crowded canvas was much regarded in its day – Frith reputedly receiving the largest sum ever given to an artist for a single work up to that time – but the Pre-Raphaelite study of 'realistic people' in unsubtle narratives is not now fashionable. 'The Railway Station' remains the classic image of the Victorian station however.

At the beginning of 1860 the main stations of London were as follows:

London Termini, 1860

Terminus	Company	Age (years)
London Bridge	South Eastern and London Brighton and South Coast railways	24
Euston Square	London and North Western Railway	23
Bishopsgate	Eastern Counties Railway	20
Fenchurch Street	London and Blackwall Railway	19
Waterloo Bridge	London and South Western Railway	12
King's Cross	Great Northern Railway	8
Paddington	Great Western Railway	6

Another, Victoria, was in the final stages of construction. In the meantime its trains terminated at a temporary wooden halt south of the Thames called Pimlico. Parliamentary permission had also been granted for a new station at Charing Cross.

The ages given in the table on p.27 are somewhat misleading as the fabric of all of these termini was virtually new. Four were newly opened or recently entirely rebuilt, and the other three had been substantially rebuilt. The most important architectural development in the previous decade was the appearance of the great iron and glass train shed. This reached its apogee in the 1860s at St Pancras. Those existing in 1860 could be said to be the experimental precursors of the greatest of Victorian engineering achievements.

With the exception of London Bridge, which, with no fewer than ten platforms, was London's first 'superstation', none of the others had more than four platforms and the majority had just two. Common practice at this time was to have one platform for departures (with the booking office) and one for arrivals (by the cab road), and to manhandle carriages from one to the other by means of transverse lines and turntables. After 1860 platforms would multiply rapidly, particularly after the introduction of bogie coaches in later Victorian times.

In 1860 London was already the world's leading railway city. After 1860 London left its competitors far behind and finished the Victorian era with an unparalleled fifteen termini (see Annexe: Station to Station).

London Bridge

It would be difficult to exaggerate the importance of London Bridge at this time. In later years the station would be almost entirely concerned with dull commuter traffic. At this time however, London Bridge was the point of departure for the South Coast resorts and the continent via Dover. The station also teemed with day trippers to Greenwich and the Crystal Palace, as well as a smattering of City-bound clerks.

In 1860 London Bridge was really two stations side by side. On the left, from the approach slope, was the South Eastern station of 1851. The undistinguished frontage was the work of Samuel Beazley, London's leading theatrical architect of the day. There was little of the dramatic here. Inside were six platforms, two each for 'Dover', 'North Kent' and 'Greenwich' line trains, the first two sets covered by a handsome arched roof, very briefly the biggest in the world, but the last a small and mangy shed. Next door was the Brighton station, a sprightly six-year-old, plain faced with a nondescript iron and glass roof behind covering four platforms, two for the main line and two for suburbia. Overall, the appearance was business-like but lacking *élan*.

The 1860 setup was a long way from the London and Greenwich days when the station was a mere yard at the end of a viaduct, without shelter or even platforms. That, however, was all that was required. Within a few years the little local line was joined by trunk routes to the south-east and the Brighton coast – British railway companies properly fulfilled their titles (which must come as a bit of a shock to our glorious American allies with their small 'Greats' and petty 'Pacifics'). In 1845 there had been an abortive if innovative attempt at a joint station; these were common up north but were never a feature in London. Inter-company rivalries scotched that idea and in 1850 a great dividing wall between the South Eastern and the Brighton sections went up and the rather nice Italianate building of the joint station, never completed in any case, came down.

South-eastern side, London Bridge station, 1851: the face of the 'plain Jane' of London's stations. (*Illustrated London News*)

Brighton side, London Bridge station, 1854: much like the other side but with quoins. (From an old guide book)

The station as it stood in 1860, although extensively altered in the following decade with the South Eastern extension to Charing Cross and the Brighton side rebuild, would not have been unrecognisable in 1940. At the end of that year however, London Bridge station was badly blitzed. Redevelopment in the 1970s swept much of the rest away. Any surviving links to the past are unlikely to survive the next round of redevelopment (the charming and discreet 'Shard' and its accompanying gewgaws which we await with glee) which will hit the station soon.

Euston Square

Although no longer the sole route to the north, Euston was still London's most important station. Long-distance travel to the Midlands, Lancashire and Scotland was the *raison d'être* of the station. Little attention was paid to suburban traffic and indeed it was not for another twenty years that even a feeble attempt was made to attract this.

In contrast to London Bridge, Euston retained its early features. The most prominent relic was the great grey stone 'Arch'. Although it was not yet hemmed in, the great clunky thing was already a terrible embarrassment to its owners. It was a great symbol – the gateway to the north, built of proper northern stone (Tripeazite from the great grim Groggly mines) – and a noble monument to the classical pretentions of the early railway magnates. But it was also completely impractical, a traffic hazard from birth.

Behind it was a more recent erection in a less straight-laced classical style – the Great Hall. This was the first station concourse and would be widely imitated in America (the concourse at Grand Central in New York is a lineal descendant). The Great Hall was the work of Philip Charles Hardwick, son of the Arch architect Philip Hardwick, and came with an ornate ceiling copied from St Paul Outside-the-Walls in Rome. Like the Arch, it looked magnificent even if it was really a little tawdry, with its plaster and string 'marble' columns. At its centre sat George Stephenson, inappropriately since Euston and its line were the product of his son Robert. Behind, a grand staircase led to the Shareholders' Meeting Room, where 'happy clappy' capitalists could celebrate – transporting tacky Brummagem wares made the LNWR a very good buy. Clustered around here were dreary waiting and refreshment rooms.

Two pairs of gloomy platforms braced the hall. The original, extended and rebuilt with roofs raised, stood to the right. To the left, 'The York', thus named because when opened in the early 1840s, this was where trains to the capital of the north departed from. No longer since the opening of King's Cross, but the name stuck.

Within a decade or so, Euston received a grandish approach from the main road with a brace of cute lodges and a set of new platforms. More followed towards the

The Arch, Euston station, 1838, showing the grand vista soon obscured. (Author's collection)

The Great Hall, Euston station, 1849: magnificent (and cheap), its loss was much worse than the gawky arch. (*Illustrated London News*)

end of the century. Despite the modernising intentions of the London, Midland and Scottish Railway (LMS) and the light-footed attentions of the Luftwaffe, the whole archaic mess soldiered on into the '60s. Today there are few remains of old Euston and none are on site – the entrance gates, Great Hall statues and the George Stephenson statue can be found at York's National Railway Museum.

Bishopsgate

The Eastern Counties Railway served a vast chunk of the country, yet its terminus at Bishopsgate was small and usually peaceful. The vast suburban empire which was to make its successor, Liverpool Street, the busiest in the capital was as yet undreamt of and long-distance traffic to the slumbering towns of East Anglia was relatively light.

Bishopsgate was a great square brick and stone lump perched high over insalubrious Shoreditch, under which name it was originally known. The name was officially changed in 1846 but the place remained Shoreditch in common parlance. The building, serviceably Italianate, was almost certainly the work of the company's engineer John Braithwaite rather than the intriguingly named Sancton Wood as is often stated. It was certainly clunky enough to be an engineering job. Wood's stations, such as Dublin's Heuston (formerly Kingsbridge), were works of art. At least the layout, with a fair-sized front yard and covered carriageway, was rational.

The platform coverings were unique: three spans of corrugated iron supported on thin cast-iron columns. Circular portholes above the side aisles and an arcaded clerestory in the centre let in some light but it still must have been gloomy – and noisy – when it rained. The station still retained its original two platforms.

The fabric dated back to the early 1840s and was already sometimes under strain. In 1862, the Eastern Counties became part of the Great Eastern Railway (GER). The new company pressed forward with plans for a new line to the City. The extension is usually explained by remoteness from the centre. However, Bishopsgate was no further out than Waterloo or Euston. The real reason lies in the poverty of the company's catchment area. East Anglia was simply not a thriving area and a scattering of country bumpkins and rural parsons did not good business make. Instead, the Great Eastern sought to develop its commuter belt. City workers, it was reasoned, required quick delivery to their destination – in other words, a centrally located station.

In the event, due to the global financial crisis (*plus ça change…*) the new extension did not arrive until 1874. The old station was soon demolished and a spiffy new goods depot was built on its site (see later). Underneath, the ancient viaduct survived. In 2010, part of Wheler Street, which runs through the site, was renamed Braithwaite Street as a tribute to the engineer, a section of whose work is to be retained.

Bishopsgate station, 1850: a busy place at any time but especially at Christmas.
(*Illustrated London News*)

Fenchurch Street

Unlike the other stations featured in this section, Fenchurch Street was always concerned entirely with short-distance traffic.

Fenchurch Street was located right in the heart of the City of London. Its frontage of yellow stock brick was quite simple, the curved profile matching the shed within. On the ground floor was a pair of booking offices, one for Tilbury-line traffic, the other for the rest. Stairways led up to a small concourse. Here were four narrow platforms under an arched iron and glass roof, alas not of clean lines. The fabric dated back only to 1853 when the station had been rebuilt under the guidance of George Berkley. Berkley, later knighted, was a foreign railway specialist working in South Africa and India and was later, prestigiously, president of the Institution of Civil Engineers.

The most notable feature of Fenchurch Street was not its buildings but its traffic. Trains of the London and Blackwall ran through the East End to the docks. These had been joined in 1850 by North London trains to the up-and-coming districts of the inner north. The Eastern Counties also operated a burgeoning suburban system from here. The station was also the terminus of the London, Tilbury and Southend Railway (LTSR), a being fostered by the Blackwall and Eastern Counties companies, but which had escaped its creators to run wild in south Essex.

For over a century, Fenchurch Street seemed stuck in a time warp. Even today, the frontage remains much as it was in those far-off days. Behind is a different story. Internal affairs were rearranged in a cosmetic fashion in 1883 and 1935 but the 1990s brought the erection of a massive office development (definitely no oil painting) over the platforms in place of Berkley's train shed.

Exterior, Fenchurch Street station, *c.*1965: although well used, the station was stuck in a time warp. (Author's collection)

Interior, Fenchurch Street station, *c.*1905: the arch of the roof matched the curve of the façade. (Author's collection)

The biggest change has been the reduction in the destinations reached from the tiniest terminus. First to go were the North London trains, diverted to Broad Street in 1865. Blackwall services came under Great Eastern auspices in 1865, and, long underused, came off in 1926. The last of the former Eastern Counties services ceased in 1949. This left just the Tilbury trains. Local services had been diverted over the Whitechapel and Bow Railway (now part of District Line) in 1902. Ten years later, in a surprise move, the London, Tilbury and Southend Railway was eaten up by the Midland Railway, a long-distance company operating out of St Pancras. Southend line services, electrified in 1962, remain the sole traffic of Fenchurch Street.

Waterloo Bridge

The South Western terminal was already very busy. As well as a flourishing long-distance trade to the ports and historic towns of Hampshire and the south-west, suburban traffic on the Windsor lines was considerable. Travellers on the latter did not include the Queen, who preferred to travel Great Western.

The station, officially Waterloo Bridge until 1882 but widely bridge-less from opening, was located on a viaduct high above the Lambeth slums. Fronting the road was a squat, quoined monstrosity with classical aspirations designed by William Tite. Tite was a proper architect, extensively involved in railway work at home and on the continent, but with church and commercial interests too. His greatest work was the Royal Exchange, the centrepiece of which is now the Bank intersection. Leading upward on either side were inclined approach roads. That to the left led to the departure side and the booking office building. Behind were four long narrow platforms under a plain iron and glass shed. Behind the existing station, new platforms, linked to the old by a metal bridge, were in the course of construction. This was the north station.

Waterloo was laid out as a through station but the planned extension to the City never came to pass. This origin could be clearly seen in 1860 with the platforms curving towards their destination and terminating immediately above Waterloo Road. Tite's front building might well have been designed to have lines pass through it, in the fashion of the *Durchbrochene Haus* of Berlin's elevated railway. The quest for the City was the overwhelming concern of the company for the rest of the century because of the considerable development of suburban traffic in LSWR territory, but it was not until the opening of the Waterloo and City tube ('The Drain') in 1898 that travellers finally had a functional link to the City.

The old station, with its long platforms and flanking roadways, was well designed. It was, however, not capable of enlargement. The north station was just the start. The year 1878 brought the south station or 'Cyprus', which, like the north, was cut off by a cab road. The Imperial theme continued in 1885 with

Waterloo Bridge station, 1848: the original core is laid bare here. (*Illustrated London News*)

'Khartoum', a suburban annexe to the north. The latter was the sole survivor of the thorough rebuilding of 1900–22 but fell victim to the coming of the now abandoned International station. Today, Waterloo is Britain's most well-used station and one of the easiest to use.

King's Cross

In 1860, the Great Northern Railway (GNR) was relatively undeveloped. Traffic was almost entirely long distance – to Scotland and industrial Yorkshire – with very little suburban trade. Additionally, the Midland Railway used King's Cross between 1857 and 1868.

Only eight years old, King's Cross was in pristine condition, with its towering yellow brick walls bright and new. The main façade fronted Euston Road where, up to 1845, had sat the monument to King George the Vile, from whom the road intersection and ultimately the station gained its name. An open arcade sat beneath a pair of vast lunettes which mirrored the arched roof within, the whole thing topped off by a rather incongruous clock. Passengers, however, entered the station from the side. This was given full architectural treatment in railway 'Italianate' and housed the GNR head office as well as the booking office.

What impressed at King's Cross were the two huge semi-circular roofs, clean of line and free of struts and ties. Uniquely these were carried on laminated timber ribs constructed of thick planks screwed together and kept in shape by iron formings. Light but strong, the technique enabled Lewis Cubitt, the station's designer, to build expansively and solidly. The roof was not without precedent,

railway-wise – Brunel's Bristol Temple Meads also had a timber
roof. Lamination under the Wiebeking system was something
new however. The standard two platforms and no fewer
than fourteen carriage sidings were covered by the
roof. The whole station was cheaply and quickly
built and was the largest in the country when
finished.

The following decades saw rapid
growth in local traffic which brought
forth a ramshackle 'suburban'
annexe to the west and a
multiplication of platforms
in the main station. At

Left: Detail of construction, King's
Cross station, 1852: lots of bits of
wood stuck together with glue, not a
good idea. (*The Builder*)

Below: King's Cross station, 1852:
like Fenchurch Street, another arched
roof, another plain front. (*Illustrated
London News*)

THE KING'S-CROSS TERMINUS OF THE GREAT NORTHERN RAILWAY.

the same time, problems with the roofing became evident. A moveable timber stage was erected and in 1868–70 the eastern train shed was renewed in metal. The western shed was dealt with in 1886–7. Despite flaws in practice, the structural use of timber was a sound idea – modern examples include beatnik Manchester Oxford Road station and the very hip Winter Gardens in Sheffield.

The Cross is next on the hit list for redevelopment. Whether the treatment will be the kitsch lashings of Liverpool Street or the brutal gouging inflicted on St Pancras, it is certain to involve multiplicities of high-class tat shops and some unpleasant surgery on the body of this venerable old dowager. Regardless, King's Cross will remain the oldest railway building in the capital that is still performing the task it was made for.

Paddington

Paddington was also almost entirely concerned with long-distance traffic at this time. Suburban traffic would grow after the Metropolitan Railway (then under construction in the far right-hand corner) gave the Great Western a welcome connection to the City.

From the road, Paddington was unremarkable. Fronting Praed Street was a retro concoction of a hotel. Round the corner, a dour Georgian-style pseudo-terrace formed the company offices with the booking hall and waiting rooms on the ground floor. Included here was the sumptuous royal waiting room, specially built for Queen Victoria.

What a contrast inside – a vast iron and glass cathedral, the like of which was to be found nowhere else on earth. The great nave was flanked by two aisles and cut through by two transepts. Brunel certainly deserved acclaim for his grand conception but largely ignored was the contribution of Matthew Digby Wyatt. An extremely cultured gentleman scholar, Wyatt was the scion of a family with an architectural record of more than two centuries. The detailing, conceived without recourse to any historical precedent, was fantastic and truly inspired.

Less inspired were the passenger arrangements. As well as the arrival and departure platforms, there were two islands, one of which was accessible only by a movable bridge. This was stored under the side platform and drawn out by chains worked by hydraulics and raised up to platform height when required. A typical over-ingenious Brunel device – a simple overhead bridge would have worked just as well.

The whole thing was enormously costly – six times the sum spent on King's Cross. But the Great Western was keen to show itself to be a solid wealthy body, most worthy of investment. Read the station as a billboard: 'Buy here'. The Great Northern, serving the self-evidently profitable industrial heartland, didn't have to try.

Paddington station, 1854: this is quite the best of all the termini, and thoroughly ahistorical. (*The Builder*)

As was the case elsewhere, late Victorian times brought a plethora of platforms. An additional shed, beating the original in size if not in detail, went up during the not-so-Great War and in 1933 the whole station got a shiny new upgrade, white with monogram. In between, and very unobtrusively, much of the wrought and cast iron was replaced by steel. A great deal of care was taken to ensure that no detail was lost. Not so careful was the big bomb which took a bite out of the offices in 1941. Despite the intrusion of the inevitable statue, Paddington remains the least changed of all the mid-Victorian stations and even manages atmosphere! Long may it continue so.

Annexe: Station to Station

No other British city ever had more than four main stations at one time. However, internationally there are comparisons to be made. The number after the city in the following indicates the number of termini in 1910, the height of the railway age.

Berlin (6)

Berlin was exceptional because, from the 1880s, long-distance traffic was funnelled into the Stadtbahn. The latter's construction halved Berlin's termini total, from a substantial ten to a paltry five, pretty much overnight. The survivors, in various historical styles, were junked after the war. Most memorable is the preserved fragment of the Anhalter. Today, there is but one – the recently opened Hauptbahnhof.

Chicago (6)

Chicago was America's railroad city. Its six historic stations were a fine selection of Vicwardian commercial architecture and engineering. Two, the North Western and Union, were rebuilt in the first quarter of the twentieth century but only the magnificent Beaux Arts Great Hall of the Union remains today.

Vienna (7)

Vienna's big six were solid affairs carried out in a variety of classical guises, the best being the gothic-style Nord. All were destroyed or badly damaged during the Second World War. The Süd is being replaced by a massive new Hauptbahnhof.

New York (7)

Most Big Apple-bound roads terminated on the Jersey or Long Island shores, with passengers proceeding to Manhattan by ferry. The unusual urban train-ferry interchange stations at Hoboken and Communipaw survive, the latter preserved.

The exceptions were something really special. Edwardian-era Pennsylvania station was a showpiece, with underground platforms and grand classical surface works, but Grand Central Terminal is truly iconic, and is the largest and most famous station in the world.

Buenos Aires (8)

Argentina was the only country in South America to have a major railway network. This was focussed on the capital. The main stations of Buenos Aires are Retiro, Once and Constitucion, all with fine historical buildings. Retiro, in a fashion akin to London Bridge (formerly), is actually three separate stations, two with preppy classical buildings, the other contrastingly folkish.

Grand Central Terminal, New York, c.1940: passengers' nirvana – meet me by the clock at Grand Central. (Author's collection)

Paris (9)

The French capital has six main termini, all originally classical in design. The Chateau-style St Lazare is the most tasteful, the Nord and Est almost as gawky as London's King's Cross, and the Lyon an exhibition fantasy. Three later additions, including the d'Orsay (part of which is now the famous art gallery), were underground affairs.

Moscow (9)

Outwardly at any rate, Moscow's stations are the least changed of any railway city. It still has all nine of its historic termini and only one has been thoroughly concretised. Those with Russian-revival buildings from the early twentieth century are the most interesting. These include the Kazansky with its squat lowering tower, the wedding cake Rizhsky and the weird Yaroslavsky.

London had fifteen termini in 1910 and today lacks but two of that number – a clear winner, then and now. Though often more interesting architecturally and with more spectacular engineering, in no other city in the world other than London did stations proliferate to such an extent.

Gare de l'Est, Paris, c.1905: much altered but this is the last of the first termini. (Postcard from author's collection)

1870: TOMORROW TO FRESH WOODS AND PASTURES NEW

South London Suburban Boom

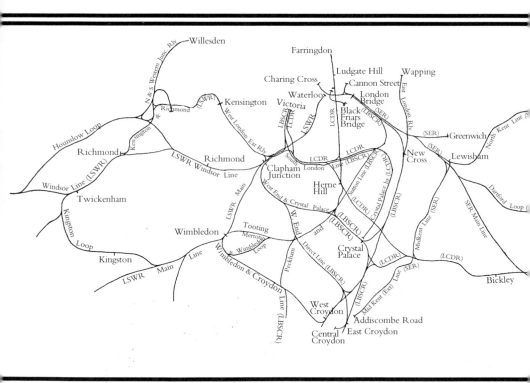

Southern suburban lines in 1870.

D uring the previous decade, London's railways had experienced unparalleled growth:

Construction of Railways in London, 1830-1950

Decade	Miles built*	Per cent of total
1830–39	42	10
1840–49	46	11
1850–59	68	17
1860–69	124	32
1870–79	47	12
1880–89	22	5
1890–99	22	5
1900–09	16	4
1910–19	7	2
1920–29	4	1
1930–39	5	1
1940–49	0	0
Total	393	100

★ *10 miles radius of Charing Cross (excluding tube railways).*

This great leap forward was concentrated in the southern sector. Of the 1860s total, 71 miles was accounted for by lines wholly or partly under the control of the southern companies. Although not all the southern companies were equally affected, it can be said that the sixties marked the creation of a dense and interpenetrating network of lines south of the Thames.

The essentials of South London railway topography were:

Dominance of suburban rather than goods or express services.
Deep penetration into the centres of London (West End and City).
High degree of duplication of destinations and routes.

The main factor determining the history and layout of South London's railways was the fact that the southern companies were resource poor. Having no industrial hinterland to generate traffic the companies inevitably turned to the possibility of a suburban bonanza. The mid-Victorian boom of the 1860s gave the companies an ample supply of capital for a spending spree. But new lines were built not just in the outskirts but also at the centre to bring the commuters as close as possible to their destinations. The picture was complicated by the existence of virtual free-for-all competition, which lead to duplication.

In the event, however, the suburban goldmine proved to be a chimera, with the south failing to grow rapidly enough to justify such great investment. The potential of the southern network was only to be released by electrification during the interwar period.

London, Chatham and Dover Railway

Of all the southern companies, the 'Chatham' owed most to the 1860s, with 12 of its 22 London miles built at this time. Indeed, the London, Chatham and Dover Railway (LCDR) was a supreme product of the greed and folly of this era. The company should never have had an independent existence – Kent had barely enough traffic to justify one company let alone two – and its story was one of wasted effort and ruin for the shareholders. But this was the era of unregulated competition and perhaps the lesson had to be learned.

The LCDR had its origins in the East Kent Railway of the 1850s – apparently a typical 'independent' local line soon to be eaten up by the local monopoly, the South Eastern. Yet the East Kent escaped its fate. Expanding rapidly, it assembled a main line from London to Dover and renamed itself the London, Chatham and Dover Railway.

At first the company gained access to the capital indirectly. However, at the end of 1860 the company brought its own rails up as far as Bickley. There followed

Cannon Street station, c.1900: although more usually frequented by city gents, commoners were also able to travel from here. (*Illustrated London News*)

Chatham side, Victoria station, *c.*1905: a wide platform for big trains, also suitable for King Edward the Obese who had his own (not very well used) royal waiting room here. (Author's collection)

running powers over the track of two semi-independent short lines and then over the Brighton's West End and Crystal Palace route to Victoria. The company had greater ambitions and before long put forward a comprehensive scheme involving lines to the West End and City (diverging at Herne Hill) and branches to Crystal Palace and Greenwich. This was put into effect immediately and the main line to Victoria was completed in the summer of 1863. The City line, including the big station at Blackfriars Bridge and the smaller but better-placed Ludgate Hill, opened the following year. The prestigious line to the Crystal Palace came in 1865. Completing the system were links to the Metropolitan's City Widened Lines at Farringdon and the West London Extension Railway near Clapham Junction. The Chatham also had a stake in the East London Railway but never operated services over it.

The Chatham's suburban lines were served at this time by a variety of locomotives, including a stud of 0-4-2 well tanks, which performed well in urban conditions. These were known as the 'Scotchmen' because, like the delectable Irn-Bru, they were made in Glasgow. They also bore the names of Scottish rivers and isles – the company's engines were not numbered until 1875. At this time, Chatham engines were neatly turned out in medium green with black bands, red and white lining, and brown underframes. Carriages were little more than primitive boxes. Third class was kept deliberately poor, dark and cold with hard wooden seats, to encourage regulars to travel (expensive) first.

With its well-positioned termini at Victoria and Ludgate Hill, plethora of stations in the suburbs (carried out in fashionable multi-coloured brick with

Blackfriars station, 1863: a good station in a bad position. (*Illustrated London News*)

gothic details), northern connections and direct access to the Crystal Palace, the Chatham seemed set to exploit the potential of the capital. However, other lines already served almost all of the company's territory. And despite the smart stations – Crystal Palace with its huge arched roofs was the most outstanding – the poor state of the company's trains and its reputation for accidents did not endear it to the public. Foreign working over the company's lines was common – the LSWR ran into Ludgate Hill, the LNWR and GWR into Victoria and the goods service was practically worked by the Great Northern and Midland. Poor profitability and vast debts sent the company into bankruptcy in 1866.

In the early 1870s the LCDR opened a rash of lines, including the most part of the Greenwich branch (the final mile or so came almost twenty years later), the Smithfield Curve, allowing Chatham trains to gain Moorgate, and a new well-planned City station at Holborn Viaduct. The '80s saw yet another new City station at St Pauls (now Blackfriars). Last, in 1892, came the Nunhead–Shortlands line, now known as the Catford Loop. In 1899 the Chatham threw in the towel and agreed to a working union with the South Eastern as the South Eastern and Chatham Railway (SECR), although the old LCDR was not totally consigned to the dustbin of history until the Grouping. The Great War brought closure of many stations and the Greenwich Park branch. What remained of the LCDR London lines went electric in 1925. The Crystal Palace branch closed in 1954. Today only faint traces remain of the old Chatham in London – a fitting end for the railway that never should have been.

Ludgate Hill station, *c*.1905: a bad station in a good position. (Author's collection)

Herne Hill, *c*.1905: a little-known junction, this was the division point of Chatham City and West End services. (Author's collection)

Crystal Palace station, 1865: the station was right by the palace but accessed by a roundabout route. (*Illustrated London News*)

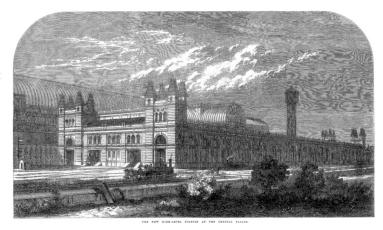

London, Brighton and South Coast Railway

Although the London, Brighton and South Coast Railway (LBSCR) had its roots in the first generation of London railways, it was not until the 1860s that it became big in the south, doubling its metropolitan track miles from 28 to 56 miles.

Before 1860, the 'Brighton' depended on running rights over the London and Greenwich to London Bridge for the last few miles into town. At the beginning of that year, its suburban lines consisted of the well-established branch to Epsom via Sutton, the feeble Croydon to Wimbledon line and the recently completed West End of London and Crystal Palace Railway. This last showed great promise but was still ending, rather sadly, south of the river at a small wooden station called Pimlico. By the end of the decade the company had an extensive suburban network and independent entry to both the West End and City.

The first act began promptly in 1860 with opening of Victoria station, the Brighton's West End terminal. A more direct line, eliminating the gradients and curves of the old West End of London amd Crystal Palace route, opened a few years later. This would ultimately supersede the London Bridge route as the Brighton's main line. The opening of Clapham Junction and connection with the West London in 1863 brought the Western show to a close. Southerly developments followed with the opening of the South London Line in 1866–7. This inner suburban line from London Bridge to Victoria was carried out in co-operation with the LCDR. In connection with the arrival of the South London, the LBSCR side at

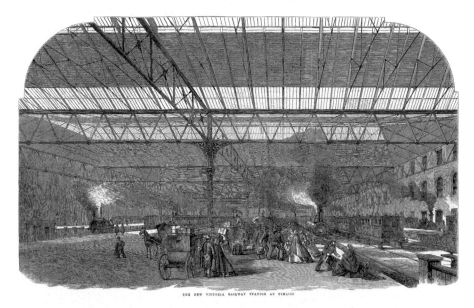

Brighton side, Victoria station, 1860: a fine site but not a fine sight, girders and string. (*Illustrated London News*)

London Bridge gained a nice new train shed to add to the hotel erected a few years previously. Connecting to the South London was the Peckham Rye to Sutton line, an archetypal suburban railway. Included in its 1868 debut was the Tooting, Merton and Wimbledon loop, which was a joint production with the LSWR. Also featuring on the 1868 show was the ill-fated branch to Central Croydon. The Brighton also had a share in the East London Railway and the West London Extension Railway which were opened during the decade. The East London included Brunel's Thames Tunnel and was not completed until 1876. The West London Extension provided a link to the northern lines.

Denmark Hill station, c.1905: this is a south London gem and has been recently restored. (Author's collection)

Wapping station, 1871: Dore style on the East London ine – the line was mainly worked by the Brighton. (*Illustrated London News*)

In 1870, power for local trains in the London area was supplied by a large range of tank engines. These came under the category 'miscellaneous' – John Chester Craven, the company's locomotive, carriage and wagon superintendent, did not believe in standardisation. His successor, William Stroudley, did, and his 'Terriers', neat 0-6-0 side tank engines liveried in yellow and named after locations on the LBSCR system, became standard fare in the metropolis by the end of the 1870s. Carriages were, as was usual at this time, fairly basic.

The LBSCR operated a large and complex suburban network from its termini at London Bridge and Victoria. Unlike the Chatham with its one-size-fits-all building, the Brighton let a thousand flowers bloom so far as its suburban stations were concerned. Chiefly these were well-built but dull edifices. However, on the London Bridge to West Croydon stretch, there were some interesting oddments such as the Tudor-style building at Anerley. The most impressive buildings were on the South London line, including the huge piles at Denmark Hill and Battersea Park. There was little foreign working over the LBSCR, although the LSWR and LCDR used short sections as part of their networks. However, the company was not in a good financial condition and had almost followed the LCDR into bankruptcy after the crash of 1866.

Subsequent development of the Brighton suburban network was relatively minor. In the 1880s, several stations received new ornate buildings (such as Forest Hill) and two minor lines south of Croydon, owned jointly with the South Eastern, were opened. In the years before the First World War, the better-used stretches were converted to overhead electric working. However, the Southern switched this to third rail in the late 1920s, when the rest of the ex-LBSCR lines were electrified. Most of the old LBSCR network remains in use today, including the Croydon–Wimbledon line, which has been taken over for light rail use.

South Eastern Railway

Although the South Eastern (SER) did not expand as much as the LCDR and LBSCR during the 1860s, the decade was an important period for the company with 13 miles, or nearly a third, of its ultimate 45-mile London network, built at this time. The routes built were particularly important for the South Eastern as they helped create a framework within which expansion could continue into the twentieth century.

At the dawn of the decade the South Eastern, like the LBSCR, relied on running rights for its access to London. In this case, however, it was not the last few miles that were problematic but a long intermediate stretch between Purley and Bermondsey. In addition to the busy London and Greenwich, whose northern end formed the approach to London Bridge, the SER had two other London branches in 1860. Most important was the straggly North Kent line along the south bank of the Thames estuary. The other, the Mid Kent Railway, was a bit of a loser. Its title was a terrible fib – it scarcely got into the garden county at all, petering out in the wastes of the southern suburbs.

The main development of the 1860s was the new South Eastern main line diverging from the North Kent near Lewisham. Completed in 1868, this was laid out for fast running rather than suburban use. As well as providing a wholly owned route to the capital, it was shorter than the previous route (vital, given the LCDR's 'air-line' to Dover). Branching off at Hither Green was the Dartford

Right: Charing Cross station, c.1905: originally equipped with another great roof that collapsed in 1905. (Author's collection)

Below: Cannon Street station, 1866: this was the pride of the South Eastern. (*Illustrated London News*)

Loop of 1866. In addition to opening up new realms of commuterdom, this line avoided the tunnels and curves of the North Kent. The Mid Kent was extended to the outskirts of Croydon in 1864 but remained unexceptional. At the centre the SER replied to the Chatham challenge with new (and better) City and West End stations at Charing Cross (1864) and Cannon Street (1866). The South Eastern was part owner of the East London Railway.

The standard SER locomotive at this time was the '118 class' of 2-4-0s: tender engines for the company made little use of tanks. These were fairly advanced for the day, although with their shelterless cabs, large drivers, polished brass work and copper-topped chimneys, they looked much the same as their contemporaries. Most interesting was the internal design. The company's locomotive superintendent, James Cudworth, had some odd ideas. In order to burn lower-grade coal instead of expensive coke, he invented a novel form of long firebox. This was divided in two by a water-filled partition. Each grate, with a separate firebox door, was fired alternately. The arrangement was superseded by the brick arch, universally used in later years. The livery was dark green with reddish-brown underframes. Carriages were variegated in appearance but most were primitive four-wheelers and all were renowned for their lack of comfort in every but the best class.

With its range of lines radiating out from London Bridge, the South Eastern had a well-used suburban system. Its London area stations, unlike those of its neighbours, were mostly clapboard and string affairs, although those on the North Kent and Mid Kent were more substantial. However, it was the new termini at Cannon Street and Charing Cross that impressed. These were something of a cultural revolution so far as the southern termini are concerned: well positioned with up-to-date engineering and trendy architecture. The earning ability of the South Eastern was about on a par with the LBSCR, but management was better and the SER managed to remain in a reasonable state during the decade. The expedient of granting running rights to the rich northerners to generate extra income was hardly resorted to at all.

After 1870 the company continued to expand at a solid rate. An extension of the Greenwich line and a branch to Bromley were built in the 1870s, while a branch to Hayes and a further extension to the Mid Kent (known as the Woodside and South Croydon, and owned jointly with the LBSCR) was built in the 1880s, with a loop through Bexley Heath to Dartford in the 1890s. Generally these lines were lightweight stuff. The end of the century saw the South Eastern effectively take over the London, Chatham and Dover Railway, its long-time rival. Changes to the system were mostly to the detriment of the latter. The former SER suburban network was mostly electrified in 1926. With the exception of the southern end of the Mid Kent (which now forms part of the Croydon Tram system) and the Woodside and South Croydon (closed in 1983), the old South Eastern network survives intact.

London and South Western Railway

In contrast to the previous three railways, the 1860s was not an important era for the South Western, with only 8 of its 1914 total of 36 London miles built at this time. Although interesting, the lines opened during that period were of secondary importance to an already well-established system.

The London and South Western Railway was one of the first batch of trunk lines to enter the capital, with its main line to Southampton being completed in 1840. Although suburban traffic had not been part of the original plan, within a decade an important branch to Windsor via Richmond had been opened. Leading off from the Windsor line was the Hounslow Loop. Altogether, this gave the South Western a considerable catchment area in the metropolis. The LSWR also then had a part share in the North and South Western Railway – a link line to the north.

The most important development for the LSWR during the 1860s was the opening of the Kingston Loop between Twickenham and Malden, which provided this important suburban centre with a direct railway link. Previously the town had been served by the present Surbiton station, some 2 miles from the centre of Kingston. Nearer to the centre was the Richmond to Kensington line. This oddity was to be of more use to 'foreign' companies than to the South Western, which utilised it as yet another loop in conjunction with the West London Extension Railway (held jointly with the LBSCR, LNWR and GWR). The Tooting, Merton and Wimbledon Railway (joint with the LBSCR) was another contemporary addition to the LSWR stable. Trains from all three new lines made a long march around to the LCDR's Ludgate Hill terminus, towards

Gunnersbury station, c.1905: once a transport hub stamped with South Western markings, this is now a grotty backwater. (Author's collection)

the construction of which the LSWR had shelled out considerably. The South Western was part owner of the West London Extension Railway.

At this time, suburban traffic was handled by tank engines, numbered not named, and mostly of the 2-4-0 arrangement. These were designed by the LSWR's mechanical engineer, Joseph Hamilton Beattie, and built by the Manchester firm of Beyer, Peacock and Co. from 1863 to 1875. Among the most efficient of the era, these tank locomotives survived the years well and two of the class remain in operational condition: at the Bodmin and Wenford Railway in Cornwall and the Buckinghamshire Railway Centre at the old Quainton Road station. However, neither has the original primitive appearance (polished brass dome and open cab). The 1870 livery was a dull red.

The LSWR differed from the other southern companies in that it had considerable long-distance traffic and a healthy freight scene. Despite its consequent financial health, the South Western, like the other southern companies, indulged in suburban lines. In this it was hampered by the lack of its own City terminus. However, the company had a secure monopoly in the south-western suburbs and really did not have to try too hard. The company's suburban stations were mostly meaty brick buildings. The nicest was the Tudor-style gem at Barnes. The order of its suburban operations contrasted with the ramshackle nature of its terminus. Although the LNWR briefly ran to Waterloo, the South Western was more often to be found in the role of an outsider on other companies' tracks, again an indication of its financial health.

Subsequently the LSWR went into a bit of a coma. The only post-1870 addition to its suburban network was the Wimbledon-Putney line of 1889. This, like the Richmond-Kensington line, was mostly used by the District. At the turn of the century the South Western awoke. The wholly owned Waterloo and City Railway, opened in 1898, finally gave the company a City terminus of its own, although in an unusual tubular form. Not long after, the wholesale rebuilding of Waterloo commenced. The completion in 1922 was marked by the unveiling of the magnificent war memorial arch forming the main entrance. By this time the bulk of the company's suburban lines had been electrified on the third rail principle. Apart from the Richmond-Kensington and Wimbledon-Putney lines which have been hived off to the Underground, the London LSWR still exists almost in its entirety.

Annexe: The Suburban Spell

London's southern suburban network is believed to have been the first of its kind in the world. Certainly no other city was of sufficient size to generate anything like it at that time. However, as has been hinted at, the south was nothing to be proud of. Indeed, the same may be said of London's suburban network throughout the ages. Possibly this is due to the lack of central control. Except for the brief Network South East (NSE) era (1986–94), London has never had a body controlling all of its suburban railways. Prior to nationalisation, these were owned and worked by individual companies, and afterwards the regions were (ir)responsible. NSE was a result of the sectorisation of British Railways and very successful it was too, bringing major investment to a number of rundown lines, a smart red, white and blue livery, and a promise of coordination. Unfortunately, privatisation splintered the network into a dozen or so pieces, and the resultant disorganisation and lack of drive is self-evident.

Matters could not be more different in France. Here suburban railways are taken seriously and big money is spent. Despite the fact that the lines are divided between the RATP (the Parisian local transport body) and the SNCF (national rail owned by the state), the Parisian system is a showpiece. Between 1969 and 1999, a series of deep tunnels were hewed out beneath central Paris, creating the five lines of the RER (Réseau Express Régional). With their ugly, if efficient, double-decker trains, these cross-city lines are the core of the French capital's suburban network. The Transilien services operating to outer suburban stations from the old termini are not to be sneered at either.

Tokyo, being Tokyo, takes everything to extremes. Here, a panoply of organisations is responsible for the greatest suburban network on earth. JR East, privatised successor to the national body in the area, runs twenty-three lines, while eight other private companies run the rest (fifty-five or so lines). There is little coordination but all are profitable and efficient. The situation is not strictly comparable however. Firstly, in contrast to the British situation, the private companies both own and work their own lines and have a variety of other interests besides. Additionally, Tokyo's suburban railways are, in general, short and light-ish in nature, and, with buses all but banished, have a monopoly in their respective areas.

The Germans invented the suburban railway as a distinct entity. Fifteen urban areas in the republic currently have an S-Bahn: short for *Stadtschnellbahn* (fast town railway). Characteristics include segregated tracks, electric operation, numbered lines and an integrated ticketing policy. The S-Bahns are operated as subsidiaries of Deutsche Bahn AG, a state-owned body run on commercial lines. The first S-Bahn so designated was Berlin in 1930, although many of the features had existed decades earlier. The S-Bahn is an efficient and evidently profitable mode of urban transport, greatly worthy of emulation.

International examples show that neither divided control nor private ownership is a block to efficient operation of a suburban network. Yet no other country in Europe has such an odd method of running its suburban railways as the franchise. With luck and good sense, the contractual system used for working the lines will follow that formerly used for maintaining them – into the dustbin of history.

London's Railway Circles

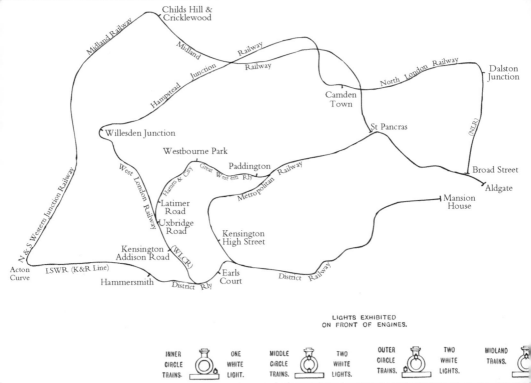

Roundabout Routes in 1880.

In 1880 there were three proper railway circles in the capital – Inner, Middle and Outer – and a fourth, here called the Super Circle, but nameless at the time:

Circular Routes, 1880

Name	Company	Route	Length
Inner Circle	Metropolitan	Mansion House to Aldgate	11m 63ch
Middle Circle	Great Western	Mansion House to Aldgate	14m 23ch
Outer Circle	L&NW	Mansion House to Broad Street	19m 44ch
Super Circle	Midland	Earls Court to St Pancras	15m 18ch

Railways were traditionally measured in chains and miles: 80 chains (ch) = 1 mile (m).

The circles were services not lines, routed over various wholly and jointly owned track and 'foreign' railways by means of running powers, all of which, with few exceptions, were also used by other services. None was a proper circle with linked ends and all were connected by their relationship with the District Railway.

The District, properly the Metropolitan District Railway, had been intended as a mere adjunct of the Metropolitan Railway and was initially worked by that company. In 1871, dissatisfied with meagre financial returns, it struck out alone. Out of economic necessity however, running from the rich northern main lines was touted for. Thus were born the Middle, Outer and Super circles. The Inner Circle was an unwelcome relic of the District's former association with the Metropolitan.

The Metropolitan Railway, 1863: the circles were a product of the first underground boom triggered by the building of the Metropolitan Railway. (From an old print)

The northern companies – Great Western, London and North Western, and Midland railways – saw potential in the destinations served by the District, which ran through the heart of the West End and City, but had existing terminal arrangements. A circular route enabled both to be served without favour. In effect, these were double-ended branch services, with the non-terminating junctions being Childs Hill (Super), Willesden Junction (Outer) and Westbourne Park (Middle). Circular routes also made economic sense because of more efficient use of personnel and stock.

The circles were not used end to end. Few passengers would have travelled the whole length – the termini were just a short walk or cab ride apart. The services primarily enabled passengers from the northern main lines to reach their destinations without a bus ride, which would be lengthy due to congestion. The Middle, Outer and Super also avoided the confusion of terminal stations and found an additional purpose as a means of transport from the western suburbs to the City and West End. The importance of this latter traffic can be seen in the impact of the Central London Railway in 1900. This gave a fast and direct connection to Oxford Street and the Bank. The Middle and Outer circles ceased within a decade – the former within a few months. The Inner was also severely affected and its electrification proceeded post haste (see 1910 section).

With well-used modern-day equivalents in mind – the North London, Gospel Oak-Barking and Circle Line – the old circles are not as odd as they might at first appear.

Inner Circle

Aldgate was the starting point of the Inner Circle service (ignore the advert – this was Mansion House-o-centric District puff). It was an unlikely terminus. Opened just four years before, it was located on the eastern fringes of the City of London – Aldgate Pump marked the beginning of the East End. With its overall roof and multiple platforms, the station was well fitted out. After being replenished with cold water (necessary for the operation of the locomotive's condensing system) and coal, which was lowered down on baskets from above, trains departed at a fair pace. Through short tunnels and brick-walled cutting, Inner Circle trains followed the route of the old city wall, past Bishopsgate, the stop for Liverpool Street, and Moorgate Street, the Metropolitan's suburban terminus, to the tangled knot of tracks at Farringdon Street.

From Farringdon to Paddington, the Inner Circle trains used the original Metropolitan Railway, the first underground railway in the world, then some twenty years old and already much the worse for wear from its daily hammering. The first section of nearly a mile to King's Cross included the only true tunnel on the circle at Clerkenwell.

Right: Inner Circle printed advertisement, 1880. (From District Railway timetable)

"INNER CIRCLE."

DISTRICT & METROPOLITAN RAILWAYS.

Trains run every TEN Minutes
(WEEK DAYS AND SUNDAYS)
BETWEEN
CITY (Mansion House Station)
and other District Stations,
AND
NOTTING HILL GATE,
BAYSWATER (Queen's Road),
PRAED STREET (Paddington),
EDGWARE ROAD,
BAKER STREET (For Madame Tussaud's),
CHANGE FOR ST. JOHN'S WOOD LINE.
PORTLAND ROAD,
GOWER STREET,
KING'S CROSS,
FARRINGDON STREET,
ALDERSGATE STREET,
MOORGATE STREET,
BISHOPSGATE AND ALDGATE.

PASSENGERS ARE BOOKED THROUGH TO AND FROM ALL STATIONS.

Below: Mansion House station, 1872: the well-configured plans will be of interest to modern users of this lost terminus. (*The Builder*)

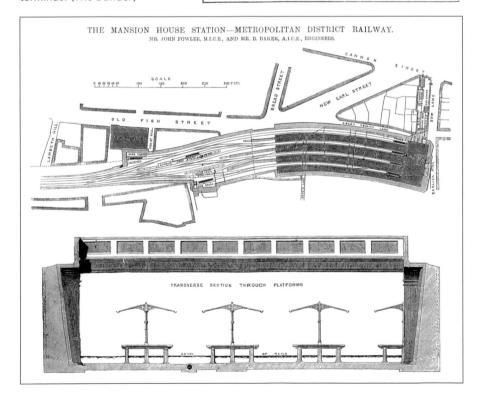

THE MANSION HOUSE STATION—METROPOLITAN DISTRICT RAILWAY.
MR. JOHN FOWLER, M.I.C.E, AND MR. B. BAKER, A.I.C.E, ENGINEERS.

TRANSVERSE SECTION THROUGH PLATFORMS

Following this, the northern straight from King's Cross to Paddington ran directly beneath the Euston and Marylebone roads (the latter allegedly the world's first by-pass). Although ingenious, the arrangement made for ventilation problems – 'blow holes' were located at intervals to scare the unwary, Marilyn Monroe-fashion. Amongst others, there were halts at Euston Square and Baker Street, the latter not yet the great junction it would one day become. At Paddington, trains for Hammersmith and the Great Western forked off right onto the Metropolitan's Western Extension.

In tight, high-walled cuttings and shallow tunnels, Inner Circle trains now ran through a high-class residential area, focussed on fashionable High Street Kensington, which provided most of the originating passenger traffic. The stations on this western arc were spacious and equipped with impressive arched roofs; thoroughly suitable for the nobs. At South Kensington the Metropolitan made an end-on junction with the District, although contemporary travellers would have noticed no obvious division.

Victoria brought a further rash of interchange. After Westminster, the line ran beneath the Victoria Embankment, construction of which had conveniently combined a new sewage system, a new road, a riverside promenade and an underground railway. At Blackfriars, the route turned inland, running under Queen Victoria Street (the Queen, if not amused, must have been flattered by this name dropping) to the Mansion House terminus. This had no fewer than seven platforms and was clearly a well-set-up affair.

South Kensington station, 1868: this engraving shows the typical appearance of stations in this area. (*Illustrated London News*)

Inner Circle trains ran every 10 minutes. Journey time was 64 minutes. The bulk, or all, of the Inner Circle services was likely provided by the Metropolitan at this time. Power was provided by 4-4-0 tank locomotives, built by Beyer Peacock Ltd of Gorton, Lancashire. The Metropolitan had forty-five of these, with a further fourteen arriving during the year. These robust and powerful little beasts, the first of which were named after Greek gods and the like, were quick off the mark but not suited to long point-to-points. The green liveried engines, with open cabs, copper-topped chimneys and polished brass domes, were provided with a novel apparatus to absorb smoke and steam while underground. Carriages were rigid eight-wheelers, finished in varnished teak, gas lit, with three classes.

The Inner Circle service was first named as such from the opening of Mansion House station on 3 July 1871, when the District began to work its own line (the Metropolitan had previously done the job), although the line had been called this from inception. This circle was unlike the others. Firstly, though those concerned might not like it, the Inner Circle was distinctly a line, not just a routing. Secondly the service was not particularly desired by either of the participants, who were more interested in pursuing their suburban dreams. The previous year Parliament had had to legally enforce the continuation of the service in the public interest. Thirdly, traffic patterns were substantially different: the service was used by passengers beginning their journey on a variety of different companies' lines not just one.

Like the others, the Inner Circle was not circular. The connection was, however, already in the works. Despite foot-dragging, the link was opened on 6 October 1884, its development hastened by the Metropolitan Board of Works, the government body then responsible for London. The sharp curves of the new line were a key feature in the Sherlock Holmes story, *The Bruce-Partington Plans*, in which a body is deposited on the line at Aldgate. Subsequently, after a short period when trains were provided by each company alternately, the clockwise service on the outer rail was operated by the Metropolitan and the anti-clockwise on the inner rail by the District. After electrification, the Inner Circle service was operated by the Metropolitan. Perhaps strangely, given that the line is self-evidently a natural unit, it was not defined as such until the 1940s, since which time, lacking competitors, it has been known as the Circle Line.

The Circle Line today is an operational nightmare. With its multiplicity of junctions and heavy usage, the slightest hitch can result in disruption across the subsurface system. Going some way to remedy this situation, the Circle was rerouted in 2009 to become a spiral. Trains currently begin at Hammersmith, loop the loop, and end at Edgware Road, then return after a rest which can help soak up any earlier delays. A complete circuit of 15 miles (22km) before this date took 59 minutes, which was no great improvement on steam-era figures. Confusing it is too for passengers with the wide range of destinations and routings. The tragedy of the Circle lies in its uncoordinated private enterprise origins. Originally

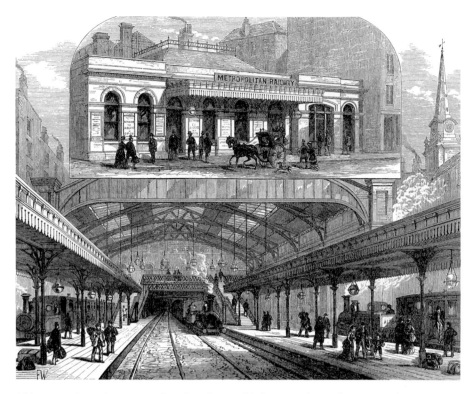

Aldgate station, 1874: not striking but thoroughly functional was the Metropolitan's City terminus. (*Illustrated London News*)

Metropolitan Railway locomotive, *c.*1885: the Beyer-Peacock was a type much used on the Circles. (Author's collection)

envisaged as a short-distance urban line with main-line feeders, such traffic was not sufficiently remunerative and the companies concerned were forced to go to the suburbs. Underused rapidly became overused, which electrification aided but did not cure. How much better would it be if the Circle Line was the only service using the Circle Line?

Middle Circle

The Great Western's entry in the great round railway stakes was the Middle Circle. The service commenced at Aldgate on the Metropolitan Railway and used the same routing as the Inner Circle as far as Paddington, before sneaking off round the side.

Here, at Bishop's Road station, Paddington's back door, Middle Circle trains passed onto Great Western home ground. The tracks from here to Westbourne Park were reserved for GWR suburban and Metropolitan trains to and from the City. Originally there had been no such separation, with Hammersmith-line trains using main-line tracks.

After having ducked under the main line, Middle Circle trains ran onto the Hammersmith and City Railway at Westbourne Park. The H&C was a product of the sixties suburban boom and was jointly owned by the Metropolitan and Great Western. The first trains were seven footers on mixed-gauge tracks but the broad was quickly stripped off. Other services using the line at this time were Metropolitan to Richmond and Hammersmith. The line was mostly viaduct-borne and, at Latimer Road, Middle Circle trains took a high-level spur, flaking off to the left. This connected through to the West London Railway at Uxbridge Road.

Middle Circle printed advertisement, 1880. (From District Railway timetable)

> **"MIDDLE CIRCLE."**
> DISTRICT & GREAT WESTERN RAILWAYS.
>
> ---
>
> Trains run every Half-hour
> (WEEK DAYS AND SUNDAYS)
> BETWEEN
> **CITY (Mansion House Station)**
> AND OTHER DISTRICT STATIONS
> AND
> **ADDISON ROAD** (Kensington),
> **UXBRIDGE ROAD** (for Shepherd's Bush),
> **LATIMER ROAD,**
> **NOTTING HILL** (Ladbroke Grove Road)
> **WESTBOURNE PARK** (Change for Great Western Main Line),
> **ROYAL OAK,**
> **BISHOP'S ROAD** (Paddington).
>
> *Through Tickets are issued between District Stations and Stations on the Great Western Main Line.*

Uxbridge Road station, c.1905: the Middle Circle tapped into a prime residential district via this station. (Author's collection)

The West London was a Great Western and North Western joint line and had originally been a simple branch to Kensington – again fitted out in mixed gauge. This had not flourished and it was not until a through connection to the south was opened at the start of the 1960s that the line had become of other than local significance. The stations in this area, Uxbridge Road (for Shepherds Bush) and Kensington, serving up-and-coming districts, received the greatest benefit from the Outer Circle service.

Not far beyond Kensington trains passed into District territory, using a short connecting line to Earls Court. This had been opened for construction purposes in 1869 but was baptised for operational use by the Outer Circle – indeed, at this time the circles were its sole user. From Earls Court to Mansion House, the Outer Circle used the 'main line' of the District Railway.

Middle Circle trains departed every half hour. The journey time was 65 minutes. Small Great Western engines, usually four-coupled and possibly equipped with condensing apparatus, were used on the service. Carriages were Great Western four wheelers, although District equivalents sometimes filled in.

First operated on 1 August 1872, the Middle Circle was an extension of the Addison Road to City service of 1864. The northern endpoint was originally Moorgate Street, the Metropolitan's not-so-grand City terminus, with Aldgate being used from 1876.

The Middle Circle was axed as a through service at the end of June 1900, a direct victim of the opening of what is now the Central Line. A truncated Aldgate–Earls Court service continued to the end of January 1905, when it became Aldgate-Kensington. An Edgware Road-Addison Road ghost, subsequently electric, lasted until 20 October 1940 when it was lost to the Blitz. Although the rest of the lines passed over are still in highly active use, the Latimer Road-Uxbridge Road viaduct link has been entirely lost. The Middle Circle can never be rejoined.

Outer Circle

The Outer Circle started at Broad Street, which was effectively the London and North Western Railway (LNWR)'s City terminus. The station was also the seat of the North London Railway (NLR)'s suburban empire. In 1880 Broad Street was a strapping, if gawky, teenager. Business was brisk and growing rapidly.

Dalston Junction station, *c.*1905: Dalston was once a huge railway complex, now all but vanished. (Author's collection)

Broad Street station, *c.*1905: North London's City station was the terminus of the Outer Circle. (Author's collection)

From Broad Street to Camden, the route passed over North London Railway metals. The first section to Dalston Junction was the NLR's City Extension. This was a well-appointed viaduct line, soaring high over Hoxton and Haggerston. At Dalston the service passed onto the original North London Railway, opened some thirty years earlier. Originally little more than a goods line to the docks, suburban sprawl had created great potential. In the previous decade, this section had been doubled and its stations upgraded in line with contemporary suburban taste. On this section, the Outer Circle bolstered existing services, rather than providing new destinations.

Outer Circle trains turned onto the Hampstead Junction line at Camden. This was owned by the LNW but, in contrast to the North London, was a poor affair, its stations poorly constructed, its engineering uninspired. After a considerable length, only partly built up, Willesden Junction was met. Confusingly, this had two sets of high-level platforms, as well as a grand array of main-line platforms, all connected together by miles of stairs and covered ways. Outer Circlers curved off left into the West London platforms. There was a considerable interchange of passengers here to and from the main line.

After bridging nigh half a dozen other lines, the West London Railway was reached at North Pole Junction. It was then but a short trip to Uxbridge Road,

---

"OUTER CIRCLE."

DISTRICT, NORTH WESTERN

AND

NORTH LONDON RAILWAYS.

TRAINS RUN EVERY HALF HOUR

(Week days only)

Between CITY (Mansion House Station) and Other District Stations, and

Addison Road.	Gospel Oak.
Uxbridge Road.	Kentish Town.
Wormwood Scrubs.	Camden Town (change for
Willesden (change for NORTH	Barnsbury and Canonbury).
WESTERN MAIN LINE, and	Islington and Highbury.
for Kilburn, Chalk Farm and	Dalston Junction (change for
Euston).	Hackney, Homerton, Victoria
Kensal Green.	Park, Old Ford, Bow, Poplar
Brondesbury (Edgware Road).	and Blackwall, and for Hagger-
Finchley Road.	ston and Shoreditch).
Hampstead Heath.	Broad Street.

Through Tickets are issued between District Stations and Stations on the North Western Main Line.

Outer Circle printed advertisement, 1880. (From District Railway timetable)

Willesden Junction station, c.1905: Wilderness Junction was a nodal point on the Outer Circle. (Author's collection)

from whence the Outer Circle route followed the same course as the Middle on the District through the West End to the City. Terminus was the south bay at Mansion House.

Outer Circle trains ran half-hourly. LNWR locomotives and rolling stock were used. The former were four-coupled tank engines fitted with condensing gear. Originally these were the Beyer-Peacock 4-4-0T types, virtually identical to those of the Metropolitan and District, of which the North Western owned a fairish stud, although Francis Webb's 'Chopper Tanks' (2-4-0T) might also have been used on the service at this time. The carriages were painted out in varnished teak to withstand tunnel conditions and were close-coupled rakes of nine.

A much wider Outer Circle line, Clapham Junction return via Finsbury Park and the East End, was proposed at the same time as what became the Inner Circle but was rejected, probably because the route followed much the same course as existing railways. The first North Western Outer Circle train ran on 1 February 1872 and was a variation on existing themes, including Broad Street–Victoria.

The Outer Circle ceased at the end of 1908. Its replacement, Willesden–Earls Court, latterly electrically operated, survived until 2 October 1940. Post-war, London Transport established a shuttle betwixt Earls Court and Kensington Olympia (the old Addison Road). Originally provided during exhibitions only but becoming full-time in 1986, this well-used but little-known service is the final successor to the Outer Circle.

Super Circle

The Super Circle commenced its steeplechase at St Pancras, the grand Midland Railway terminus, thence running up the main line to the Childs Hill and Cricklewood station. On this inner stretch St Pancras services were augmented by through trains to Moorgate Street on the Metropolitan, which provided the other City connection.

At Childs Hill the service veered off the main line onto the Midland's Acton branch. This line was opened soon after the main as a goods link to the south and was originally owned by the Midland and South Western Junction Railway Company, a worked line of the Midland and soon eaten up by it. On this stretch were the only stations solely served by the Super Circle: Dudding Hill and Harrow Road.

Right: Super Circle printed advertisement, 1880. (From District Railway timetable)

Below: Dudding Hill station, c.1905: Dudding Hill was one of the few stations only served by the circles. (From an old postcard)

"MIDLAND ROUTE TO ST. PANCRAS."

DISTRICT & MIDLAND RAILWAYS.

FREQUENT TRAINS

(Week days only)

Between CITY (Mansion House Station) and Other District Stations, and

Acton.	Finchley Road.
Harrow Road (for Harlesden.)	Haverstock Hill.
Dudding Hill (for Church End, Willesden).	Kentish Town (change for Highgate Road, Junction Road, Upper Holloway, Hornsey Road, Crouch Hill and South Totten- ham).
Child's Hill and Cricklewood.	
Welsh Harp.	
Hendon.	Camden Road.
West End (for Killburn).	St. Pancras.

Passengers change at CHILD'S HILL, KENTISH TOWN, or ST. PANCRAS (AS DIRECTED by Midland Company's Staff, at either of those Stations) for MIDLAND MAIN LINE Stations.

Through Tickets are issued between all District Stations and Stations on the Midland Main Line.

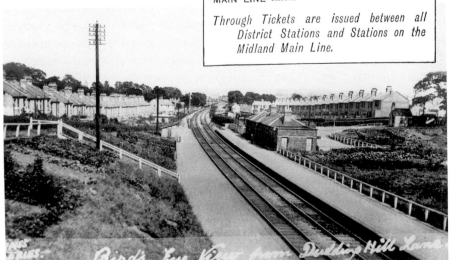

Midland Railway, St. Pancras Station.

St Pancras station, c.1905: this was the terminus of the Super Circle, amongst other more minor things. (Author's collection)

Trains passed onto the North and South Western Junction Railway (N&SWJR) at Acton Wells. The N&SWJR was owned by an independent company, but had been leased by the London and North Western, Midland and North London railways since 1871. Its primary service was North London from Broad Street.

At South Acton, London and South Western Railway territory was entered. First was the line to Gunnersbury. From Bollo Lane to Acton Lane junctions, trains used the Acton Curve. This was built specially for the Super Circle service and was only ever used by the Midland and its successors. Trains now used the LSWR's Richmond and Kensington line. This was opened to catch some of the traffic in this up-and-coming area. However LSWR services were circuitous and it wasn't until the District entered the area at the end of the 1970s that the line became of any importance.

West of Hammersmith, Super Circle trains came onto the District Railway-owned section. The Super Circle terminated at Earls Court. Ordinary District trains provided a link through to the West End and City.

The service ran fourteen times each way per day. Journey time was 45–56 minutes. Midland locomotives and rolling stock were used. The locomotives were possibly Beyer Peacock 4-4-0 types, similar to those in use on the Metropolitan and District.

The Super Circle had commenced in May 1878 but was to prove short-lived, ceasing at the end of September 1880. This was largely the result of the opening of the Metropolitan's extension to Harrow. Other factors may have been the inadequacy of connections at Childs Hill. A remnant of the Super Circle survived in the various services provided over the Acton branch until Edwardian times. Except for the Acton Curve, all lines remain in use, some only for goods.

Annexe: Right Round, Round, Round

Circular services other than the London circles were not unknown in Britain. In London, the Kingston Loop, beginning and ending at Waterloo, is well known; while up north the Great Northern operated a West Yorkshire Circle, Leeds to Leeds via Dewsbury. Circular railways, however, were relatively rare, the only notable examples being the Glasgow Subway (a highly interesting cable-worked line), and the coastal route to North Shields on the Newcastle electrics.

Abroad, ring lines were common in intra-city networks. In Australia, Melbourne had both an Inner and an Outer Circle, and Sydney has an underground City Circle. Disappointingly, the former were little more than short non-radial branches and the latter a large terminal loop. The elevated Union Loop in Chicago is also a glorified turning circle. On the subcontinent, Delhi has a ramshackle Ring Railway, while Kolkata has a surprisingly well-upholstered Circular Railway, as also had Karachi. Oslo's T-Baneringen and Moscow's Koltsevaya line are also round. Perhaps the most well-used circle is Tokyo's Yamanote line, ridden by some 3½ million passengers per day – considerably more than the entire London Underground.

Paris is well known as a city of ring railways. The equivalent of the Inner Circle was the Petite Ceinture. Built in stages from 1852–67, the line pretty much followed the line of fortifications. The distance was 32km (20 miles) with a journey time in 1914 of 1 hour 29 minutes. The Petite Ceinture was closed for local passenger traffic in 1934, rendered obsolete by Metro lines 2 and 6 (which were originally intended to be a continuous circular line), but, in part, remained in occasional use until recently for stock transfers and the like. The equivalent of the Outer Circle, but much more 'outer' than any London route, was the Grande Ceinture. Built in 1877–86 and running from Noisy-le-Sec to Versailles and back again, the Grande Ceinture was essentially a goods transfer link. 114km (71 miles) in circumference, in 1914 the journey time (with changes) was between 5 and 5½ hours. Like its smaller counterpart, the line was closed for passengers in the 1930s but is still open for goods.

Berlin, however, is the big ring railway winner. The deluxe Ringbahn, which at its height was four tracked throughout, was built in 1867–77. Locally the line is known as the *Hundekopf* (dog's head) due to its profile on a map. The ring was shut down during the Berlin Wall era but has been reopened and now hosts a regular service of electric passenger trains. A complete circuit of 37.5km (23 miles) takes

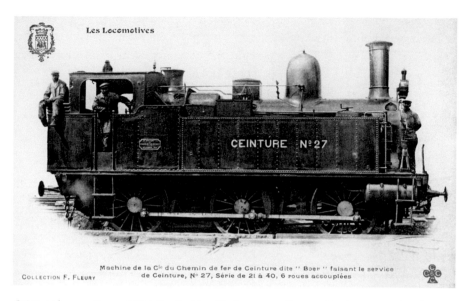

Ceinture locomotive, *c.*1905: the Parisian Circle was a railway not just a service. (Author's collection)

59 minutes. The German capital also boasts a less well-known and much less well-used line. The Berlin Outer Ring (Berliner Außenring (BAR)) was built in 1951–61 by the East German government to circumnavigate West Berlin. Amusingly, its swish double-deck trains were known as Sputniks. Apparently it was never possible to go all the way round on one train but in the mid-1990s the entire 125km (77 miles) long line could be done in four stages, with the journey time being about 3 hours. It is not now possible to outer circle Berlin on regular local trains, although all sections of the BAR are still in use.

A well-planned inner ring railway is vital to an efficient urban transport system, while an outer line is useful for avoiding congestion in goods and long-distance traffic. Interestingly, it is understood that Transport for London intends to use the compass point lines (north, east, west and south) to put together a circular routing. Sensible fellows!

London's Railway Hotels

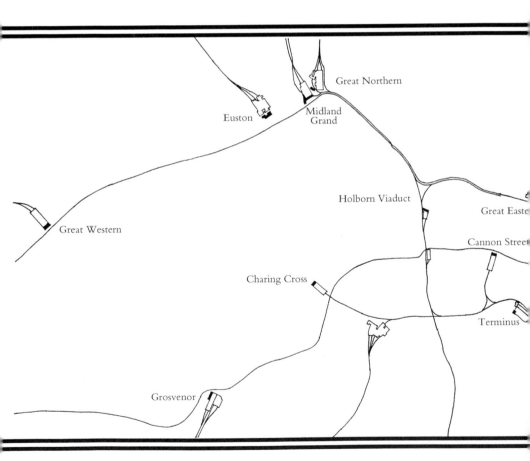

London's railway hotels in 1890.

By the 1860s, the railway hotels were the standard accommodation for visitors to the Imperial City. From 1881, this supremacy was challenged by the new giant hotels of Frederick Gordon and his imitators. The railways made a rather weak response to this and by 1890 were beginning to be seen as rather dowdy and old-fashioned. This trend would reach a peak in the following decade with the opening of the Ritz and Savoy. Yet at this point the railway hotels were still some of the best hotels in London.

London's Railway Hotels, 1890

Hotel	Station	Rooms
Cannon Street Hotel	Cannon Street	84
Great Northern Hotel	King's Cross	100
Great Western Royal Hotel	Paddington	112
Euston Hotel	Euston	140
Terminus Hotel	London Bridge	150
Great Eastern Hotel	Liverpool Street	160
Holborn Viaduct Hotel	Holborn Viaduct	170
Grosvenor Hotel	Victoria	300
Charing Cross Hotel	Charing Cross	340
Midland Grand Hotel	St Pancras	400

Not all of these were railway owned – indeed most were out of railway control at some point in their lives. The point was that they were immediately adjacent to a terminus and usually formed an integral part of its fabric. This latter point is particularly important because the London railway hotels were not particularly significant as hotels: by 1890 they were just some of the excellent but essentially middle ranking concerns in the capital (unlike in provincial cities where they usually remained top of the range). Their interest lies instead in their contribution to the external appearance of London's termini. Without the device of a fronting hotel, a station could be clumsily unattractive or untidy – as at Waterloo and Fenchurch Street.

Commonly, British railway hotels were opened and, at first, run by companies separate to, but associated with, those owning the railway itself. However, this arrangement was soon found to be unsatisfactory, as indeed was leasing out the hotel. Railway companies in Britain found affairs to be much better run when everything was done 'in house'. Public service, as well as profit, was the keystone of the railway hotel.

Nationalisation found the state the owner of dozens of major and minor enterprises up and down the country. Unlike the railways, these were highly profitable. Despite this (or perhaps because of it) the remaining British Transport Hotels were shamefully sold off in 1983. Some have found new and better lives, but others are notoriously expensive and shabby.

Cannon Street Hotel

In terms of the number of beds, this was the smallest of London's railway hotels but in the City overnight accommodation was less important than space for assignations. The most impressive meeting room was the Great Hall on the first floor, seating 1,000 and fitted out with Corinthian columns, a fine ceiling and a musicians' gallery. In 1920, the Great Hall achieved some fame as the birthplace of the Communist Party of Great Britain.

Despite this eccentricity, Cannon Street had the archetypal layout of a railway hotel. The building as a whole formed the frontage of the station, closing the great arch of the train shed. The ground floor was devoted to railway usage (booking office, etc.) and the first floor to dining, with bedrooms above. From outside the building was a typical ornate slab, here of brick, terracotta and cement ('artificial stone') carried out in the 'French' style favoured by Edward Middleton Barry, an architect of distinction whose most notable work was the Royal Opera House, Covent Garden. The high pitched roof was flanked by tiny turrets based on the spire of nearby St Mary Abchurch. Opened in May 1867, it was originally run independently but was later taken over directly by the South Eastern Railway.

Cannon Street Hotel, c.1905: a spiky monster in the City, a real loss to the capital's architectural heritage. (Author's collection)

Closed in 1931, the old hotel was converted into offices (a typical fate) and renamed Southern House. During the Blitz the upper floors were burnt out. Post-war, these were reinstated in a half-hearted fashion. The remains were demolished in 1963 and were replaced by a massive slab of offices, which was itself replaced in the 1990s.

Great Northern Hotel

Smaller and dowdier than its flamboyant neighbour St Pancras, the Great Northern Hotel was solid and dependable with a devoted clientele of Yorkshire businessmen and their families. In its day the Great Northern was one of the best. By 1890, it was still a good hotel but had long been surpassed as one of the greats.

Opened at Easter 1854, the building was designed by Lewis Cubitt, who also worked on the passenger station (a rare combination). The hotel stood apart from the station – an older layout than that of Cannon Street. The principal feature was the curved plan, due not to aesthetic considerations but to the old road layout (Pancras Road running round the back). The appearance of the building has been likened, not unfairly, to a London terrace and indeed domestic housing was Cubitt's main field of work. The yellow stock brick and white stone fixtures match the station and are by no means unpleasant to look at. Especially over the

Great Northern Hotel, c.1905: this gently curved building was a mellow retreat for the stressed tyke. (Author's collection)

crescent-shaped garden that formerly separated the twain. The Great Northern was the cheapest of the railway hotels to construct and one of the best investments as it has lasted for 150 years.

By the end of the last century, the Great Northern Hotel was rather run down and a bit scuzzy but very atmospheric, and it is this time that a song by Jude, a UK Indie band, commemorates. Shortly thereafter came closure and rebuilding. The ground floor has been hollowed out as a pedestrian arcade and the upper floors are to be refurbished as a 'luxury boutique' hotel which will reopen in time for the 2012 Olympic Games.

Great Western Royal Hotel

Although small in terms of rooms, the Great Western Hotel was born big and has remained so throughout its long life; habitués have been merchants, megastars and the like, rather the industrial hoi polloi of King's Cross.

This was the first of the proper railway hotels. Unlike its predecessors, the Great Western was large and flashy and, when opened on 9 June 1854, was unlike anything seen before. The French château-style exterior, stucco-clad and topped by mansard roofs and corner turrets, was the most fashionable in the capital and was the work of Philip Charles Hardwick of Euston Great Hall fame. Decorations included a full array of statuary on the pediment – demure English maidens,

Great Western Hotel, c.1905: the Great Western Hotel was later Royalised, fitting its palatial style. (Author's collection)

semi-naked native ladies, cherubs and elephants, llamas, beehives and telescopes, the whole kit and caboodle – sculpted by John Thomas (no laughter please – he did his stuff all over the Houses of Parliament, a real noted member). The inside was equally sumptuous, coming to a head in the luxurious 'coffee room'. The layout was also revolutionary. For the first time in London, the hotel was not physically separate from its station, but stood at the head of the platforms, an arrangement which was to become standard. Perhaps the most notable resident was the appalling Second Duke of Buckingham and Chandos, a lecherous old bankrupt, who died here in 1861.

The hotel was leased out to a separate owning company until 1896, when it became a proper railway hotel. Such an arrangement was common but by no means obligatory. In the mid-1930s the place was modernised, sadly losing the galumphing giants on the façade but gaining direct access from the station concourse. It is now known, prosaically, as the Hilton London Paddington.

Euston Hotel

The Euston Hotel was a plain place, already rather elderly in parts, but with an excellent reputation.

Euston had the distinction of having the first railway hotels in the world. These were two matching buildings, four storeys with slapped-on stucco, either side of

Euston Hotel, c.1905: the Euston was a bit of a mess outside but its innards met with approval. (Author's collection)

the approach from Euston Road. To the west was the Victoria, a 'dormitory' for packing in poorer folks, which opened in September 1839. Following in December was the more luxurious Euston, designated for first-class use. Like the famous portico opposite, these simple but functional buildings were designed by Philip Hardwick. The location of the hotels – standing apart from the station – was a typical early feature. By 1890 the two hotels had been linked by an ugly new block (of 1884) and united as the Euston Hotel. Held responsible for the joining section was J.B. Stansby, the company's engineer; most of the work, however, was done by a J. Maclaren, who, perhaps wisely, disclaimed paternity.

The 1930s plan for Euston saw no place for the old hotel. However the building was reprieved and despite war damage soldiered on until closure on 13 May 1963, a sad event and very much the end of an era. Shortly thereafter the whole area was redeveloped. Unlike the station, whose gates and statues have been relocated, there are no memento mori of the old hotel.

Terminus Hotel

The hotel at London Bridge was a very minor affair, of no particular interest and not at all popular; although near the City it was not near enough, being on the edge of Bermondsey with its unpleasant trades and even more unpleasant personages.

London Bridge station, 1905: the block in the centre is the old Terminus Hotel. (Author's collection)

The Terminus Hotel was opened back in 1861 and was owned and operated entirely independently of the London, Brighton and South Coast Railway to whose portion of London Bridge station it was attached. A plain-ish brick building, it stood at the right-hand corner of the station. The position, up front but offset from the main flow, was repeated at Liverpool Street and Victoria. The architect was Henry Currey, who worked on St Thomas' Hospital opposite the Houses of Parliament. If its style was no great shakes and its location was not hot, the hotel had all the usual facilities. In addition to the obligatory 'coffee room', also served up were a library, a room for billiards and a smoking room, as well as a dining room specially reserved for the lovely ladies.

In the event, the Terminus Hotel closed in 1893, the first railway hotel in the capital to close, deprived of its long-distance trade by Charing Cross and Victoria. It shared the regular fate, being converted to offices for the Brighton line. As such it endured until destroyed by bombing in 1940.

Great Eastern Hotel

The Great Eastern Hotel was the latest addition (May 1884) to the range of railway hotels in London. Although not comparable in size to the sexy new West End monsters, it was certainly similar in comfort and grandeur. In addition, it was in the City, where good accommodation was rare.

The Great Eastern was attached in an odd and unsatisfactory way to its station. The hotel post-dated the station and had to fit in with existing arrangements: the access road, which unhelpfully bisected the ground floor, and railway sidings, which cut into the basement. The building was the work of Charles Barry Jnr (son of Sir Charles, architect of the Houses of Parliament, and brother of Edward, of Cannon Street) and his son Charles Edward. Carried out in warm red brick with stone details such as crow-stepped gables and small turrets above, the appearance was somewhat marred by shops that occupied the ground floor. Internally the main feature was the 'coffee room', with a magnificent dome of coloured glass.

Subsequently, the hotel was extended at the turn of the century, filling up on the Bishopsgate side. The new addition by Colonel Robert William Edis (who also worked on the Hotel Great Central, the final addition to the London railway hotel clan), cunningly matched the original perfectly. The new section, known as the Abercorn Rooms, included the sumptuous Hamilton Hall with its fine plasterwork and the wonderful wood-panelled Abercorn Bar. For the Freemasons' sinister rites was provided the bizarre Greek Temple. Post-war, the GER was pretty grim and remained so after privatisation in the mid-1980s. In the millennium year, however, the hotel was made respectable again by Conran and Partners. The 'Andaz Liverpool Street London Hotel' (as per its website – has

Great Eastern Hotel, c.1905: otherwise known as the Liverpool Street Hotel, this is a stylish building now in good hands. (Author's collection)

no one heard of commas?) combines the best of Vicwardian charm with Terence Conran's characteristic restrained modernity.

Holborn Viaduct Hotel

Forming the frontage to the Chatham's City terminus, the Holborn Viaduct was, like Cannon Street, an important meeting place and, as per the Great Eastern, housed a Masonic lodge.

Opened in December 1877, some three years after the passenger station, the building's monumental Portland stone façade was designed by Lewis Henry Isaacs. Isaacs was a very competent commercial architect as well as a Conservative MP and author on architectural matters, who, with his partner Henry L. Florence, worked on Holborn's old Town Hall and the Connaught Hotel. Giant Corinthian pilasters and small shields of the arms of the cities and towns served by the LCDR were features. Inside, the main feature was the 'coffee room' (restaurant), the most

THE SMOKING-ROOM OF A FAMOUS CITY RESTAURANT

DRAWN BY F. MATANIA

A stranger unaccustomed to the ways of London would be considerably astonished were he to drop in at the splendid restaurant of the Holborn Viaduct Hotel, the property of Messrs. Spiers and Pond. The crowded luncheon-room has its own interest, certain tables being devoted to well-known City men; Mr. John Morgan Richards and several American friends, for example, are frequently to be seen at one of these tables. The interest, however, is centred in the smoking-room. There for a few brief moments many of the smokers may be seen playing draughts and dominoes with a zest that would almost make one suspect that it was the players' sole interest in life. But the cigar finished, the games are quickly abandoned and the huge oak-panelled room is empty, the strenuousness finding its outlet elsewhere

The smoking room, Holborn Viaduct Hotel, 1906: the railway hotels were social centres as well as providing overnight accommodation. (Unidentified journal)

important feature of the Victorian hotel, here decked out in Mexican onyx marble with a 'carton pierre' (glorified papier-mâché) ceiling. The kitchens were located on the top floor. This had the advantage that cooking smells did not permeate residential areas but the disadvantage was that food was cold by the time it got to the table. This was an odd choice for Spiers and Pond, the firm that ran the hotel, who specialised in railway catering.

The Holborn Viaduct Hotel was requisitioned for use by the government in 1917. Post-war it became offices for W.T. Henley, a well-known manufacturer of telegraph and other cables, before being destroyed by bombing in May 1941. The ruins were cleared away at the start of the sixties for a brand new block, now itself history.

Grosvenor Hotel

At this time the Grosvenor Hotel was completely independent of the London, Brighton and South Coast Railway, whose station it adjoined at Victoria. Reflecting this was a name which, uniquely amongst London hotels, was decidedly non-railway, taking the surname of the dukes of Westminster, the local lords of the manor, rather than that of station or company. Patronage was decidedly of the better quality.

J.T. Knowles's busty edifice of 1861 personified mid-Victorian prosperity. The whole was carried out in mild brown brick with Bath stone and matching stone-effect cement details. James Thomas Knowles specialised in mansions for the magnificent. His son, also a James, was more famous, hobnobbing with the great

Grosvenor Hotel, c.1905: the stereoscope was an early form of 3D – this is an unusual souvenir of Monsieur's stay in London. (Author's collection)

and gorgeous of the day. Included in the façade were roundel icons of famous Victorians, including Queen Victoria and Prince Albert (not in a can), by a Mr Dayman. Inside was a magnificent entrance hall and grand staircase. Sadly the marble columns were *scagliola* (fake), but this was quite common as it avoided the massive weight of real marble.

Towards the turn of the century the LBSCR was forced to buy up the hotel because of its management's obstructive attitude to station rebuilding plans. It was then let to Gordon Hotels Ltd, which brought the hotel up to standard and reopened it on 10 December 1900. A 150-room annexe to the hotel fronting the rebuilt station was erected in 1907–8. From the 1920s onwards, Victoria was the station for international services and the hotel's clientele became more cosmopolitan. Privatised in 1983 (it had only come into British Transport Hotels' hands in 1977), the hotel survives as one of the best of its type and retains the grand entrance hall and show staircase.

Charing Cross Hotel

At this time the Charing Cross Hotel had an extensive international patronage, for this was where cross-Channel services then terminated. Fares were very reasonable for the accommodation and location offered.

Charing Cross Hotel, *c*.1920: the Charing Cross is another great slab – the Cross itself is front and centre. (Author's collection)

Like the Grosvenor, the Charing Cross Hotel was a product of the prosperous 1860s, opening on 15 May 1865, a year or so after the station itself. Like Cannon Street, which it closely resembles, it was designed by E.M. Barry. Here, however, the floors were more tightly packed and meeting space mostly eliminated to give a much higher number of rooms: some 250 originally. In 1878 this figure was raised by the addition of a ninety-room annexe on Villiers Street connected to the original building by an overhead walkway. The Renaissance style façade of white brick with terracotta and cement details was topped by fashionable mansard roofs and spirelets. The best room was the dining room with its fine domed ceiling and intricate plasterwork. Balconies at the back permitted romantic residents to look out over the trains. Included in Barry's work was a replica of the medieval Eleanor Cross. At 70ft high and constructed of Portland stone with red Mansfield stone and Aberdeen granite details, this was a worthy addition to London's street scene.

The Charing Cross Hotel survives in use today with many of its Victorian features intact, although externally it is somewhat altered due to the destruction of the top floors during the Blitz. The hotel came into commercial ownership in 1983. The cross itself was recently restored. The hotel could do with the same comprehensive treatment.

Midland Grand Hotel

The Midland Grand Hotel at St Pancras was one of London's swankiest hotels at this time. Its architecture was perhaps a little dated by this point but there was nothing wrong with its service, which remained immaculate.

This is undoubtedly the most notable of London's railway hotels and indeed Sir George Gilbert Scott's gothic masterpiece is world famous. Although famously mistaken for a church (no surprise given the unchurch-like appearance of the St Pancras churches, New and Old), Scott's models were largely secular, including the Cloth Hall at Ypres. Opened on 5 May 1873, five years after the station, the hotel was not fully complete until four years later. At nearly half a million pounds this was the most costly of the railway hotels and at the time of its opening was one of the biggest and most opulent in London. The building was a huge mass of warm red brick and stone – it was to have been even larger but two floors of offices were omitted when the Midland decided to keep its head office in Derby – and featured superb detailing both inside and out. Most spectacular is the Grand Stair with its decorative ironwork and figurative wall paintings. Despite the medieval cast, the latest technology (lifts and central heating) was employed.

The Midland Grand Hotel closed on 19 April 1935 and was converted into railway offices. These were vacated in 1985 after the politically inspired assassination of British Transport Hotels. After an incredible renovation programme spanning almost three decades, the St Pancras Renaissance Hotel reopened on 5 May 2011.

Midland Grand Hotel, c.1890: the Midland Grand was the biggest and best of all the railway hotels in London, but it still needed puffing. (Advertisement from unknown source)

MIDLAND GRAND,
LONDON.
WILLIAM TOWLE, Manager.

The **MIDLAND GRAND** is designed and arranged to meet the requirements of those who desire either the most sumptuous Apartments or a modest Bachelor's Bedroom ; and the Cuisine and Wine List will be found to embrace the elegance of the French Cuisine and the choicest Vintages, and the simplest meals with the wine of the Gironde or the Rhone at one shilling the half-bottle.

The **MIDLAND GRAND** forms the Terminus of the Midland Railway, whence Express Trains depart for Scotland, Manchester, Liverpool and all principal Manufacturing Towns.

The **MIDLAND GRAND** *charges for Attendance and Gas have been abolished.* One Hundred Rooms at **3s. 6d.** and **4s.** per day, inclusive. Board, Apartments, &c., **10s. 6d.** per day for the Winter.

The **MIDLAND GRAND** has Passenger Elevators, Electric Light, Telegraph, Telephone to Theatres and business centres. Special service of comfortable Broughams, at very low fares. Table d'Hôte open to non-residents.

For the increased comfort of ladies and families visiting London, the Ladies' Coffee Room is now open. It is on the first floor and en suite with the Music, Reading, Drawing and Billiard Rooms. The corridors are well-warmed and ventilated ; the service is the best in London, and the tariff, which is exceptionally low, is the same as in the General Coffee Room.

The Midland Omnibuses will meet Families coming to the Midland Grand Hotel.

Within Shilling Cab-fare of important business and West End centres and nearly all theatres. Close to Euston and King's Cross.

The QUEEN'S HOTEL, LEEDS, MIDLAND HOTEL, DERBY, and MIDLAND HOTEL, MORECAMBE, *are under the same Management.*

£8

Annexe: Such a Lovely Place

In London, eleven of the ultimately fifteen termini had a hotel attached at some point. Of those without, only Waterloo was a true mainline station. Elsewhere in Britain, the hotel was a feature of the railway station of almost every major town and city. The larger affairs were mostly dumpy and seldom artistic – an exception was the North Western Hotel in Liverpool, designed by Alfred Waterhouse, the most prolific of Victorian architects. Of note were the Caledonian and north British monsters in Glasgow and Edinburgh, and the Midland Hotel, Manchester – the ultimate in Edwardian sophistication. The port city hotels were particularly well liked: the Royal Station Hotel in Hull even has a poem by Philip Larkin. In smaller locales, the railways mostly purchased pre-existing properties, and those that were purpose-built seldom adjoined the station. Many country and beach resorts also had railway-owned hotels, usually well away from the station. Most famous was the elite Gleneagles Hotel. Unlike in London, building continued into the interwar years – the art deco Queens Hotel in Leeds and the classic Midland Hotel at Morecambe date from this era.

Ireland, generally speaking, followed the British pattern. All were modest in size, the country hotels being particularly charming. Those in the north were sold off in 1966, while the former railway hotels in the republic remained in state ownership until 2006.

Elsewhere, railway hotels were rare. Continental European stations did not generally include overnight accommodation. An exception was Paris, where the Gare St Lazare and the Gare d'Orsay had hotels, both now closed. Further afield, the successors to the Japanese National Railways run an extensive hotel business. These appear to be conventional hotels not associated with a railway station as such.

274. – PARIS. – L'Hôtel Terminus à la Gare St-Lazare

Hotel Terminus, Paris, c.1905: squatting like *un grand crapaud*, the hotel wore the same high fashion clothing as the station behind. (Author's collection)

In the United States, the railways established enormous hotels at scenic locations, especially in the mountains. These were often provided with their own stations and even their own branch line. Most famous was the Greenbrier at White Sulphur Springs, West Virginia, where the Presidents' Cottage is a tourist attraction and where the nuclear war bunker for Congress was located. In the west, the Harvey Houses and their rivals were essentially eateries which sometimes featured lodgings. These usually formed an integral part of the station.

The railway-owned hotel reached its apogee in Canada. Those of the Canadian Pacific were most famous, but the Grand Trunk and its nationalised successor, Canadian National, also had a large chain. The urban hotels were huge, often carried out in the Château style, which has become a national speciality. The best is the impressive Château Frontenac in Quebec City, as seen in Hitchcock's *I Confess*. Notable also is the Queen Elizabeth Hotel in Montreal, scene of John Lennon's 'bed-in', whose guests range from Fidel Castro to the Dalai Lama and, of course, Liz herself. The resort hotels were also lovely places, particularly those in the Rocky Mountains – the noble Banff Springs Hotel and the rival Jasper Park Lodge, a sprawling winter wonderland. All ultimately fell to the Canadian Pacific, who spun the chain off in 2001.

As has been seen, true railway hotels – owned and operated by the railway and forming part of the station layout – were very rare outside Britain. As an idiosyncratic feature of the British railway scene, the railway hotels deserve to be better known.

1900: WITH PEACOCK'S EYES AND THE WARES OF CARTHAGE

London's Goods Depots

London's goods depots in 1900.

At the turn of the century the railways were *the* method of long-distance transport for goods. This was the classic era of the goods depot. There were then ten 'biggies', arrayed like a string of (grubby) pearls around the capital.

London's Main Goods Stations, 1900

Station Company

Station	Company
Bishopsgate	Great Eastern
Bricklayers Arms	South Eastern and Chatham
Camden	London and North Western
Commercial Road	London, Tilbury and Southend Railway
King's Cross	Great Northern
Marylebone	Great Central
Nine Elms	London and South Western
Paddington	Great Western
St Pancras	Midland
Willow Walk	London, Brighton and South Coast

Although there were differences in terms of the specific layout and types of goods handled, all did pretty much the same sort of work. This was basically the transfer of goods from rail transport to horse-drawn vehicles and vice versa. The horse was the key element here. The typical goods depot was positively buzzing with them (literally, as they attracted one or two flies). The railway-owned horse-drawn delivery and collection services (cartage) were a well-established part of London street life. Equally the decks were awash with workers. Great numbers were required for the largely manual work involved in packing, unpacking and moving the various packages and boxes. Men and horses, but few locomotives, as these were a potential fire hazard. Moving wagons was usually performed by hydraulic capstan (a lovely piece of Victorian machinery) or, more rarely, by horse.

Great Western Railway van horses, *c.*1890: the delivery horse was the linchpin of the whole railway goods system. (Illustration in a contemporary publication)

(650)‾	London and North Western Railway.						GOODS INVOICE.		Pro. No

London and North Western Railway goods invoice: each item was accompanied by a document such as this – a very paperwork-heavy system. (Author's collection)

Capstan working at Camden goods depot, c.1935: the railway goods system was heavily dependent on cheap manual labour. (Author's collection)

The heart of the goods depot was the goods shed, where small- and medium-sized items, the common stock of the goods depot, were handled. The yard, on the other hand, was for larger items and bulk goods. The yard usually had an area for goods not handled by the railways' own delivery services – the 'mileage sidings' (called this as the sender or recipient was only billed for the distance travelled on the railway). All this activity took place behind closed doors – or rather, towering walls, as these were a prominent security feature – at peculiar hours: most traffic arrived and departed during the hours of darkness in order not to conflict with passenger movements.

Anything you wanted, anything you needed – the railway did it, providing everything required for the life of the capital's inhabitants. Also, as part of the railway goods system, they brought in perhaps half the income of the railway companies. Little-known even in their heyday, the goods depots played their part in the daily life of London for more than a century, yet today even the buildings have all but disappeared.

Bishopsgate

Bishopsgate, with its multi-layered structure and variegated colouring, bore a passing resemblance to a large dish of lasagne. The yard and the goods shed were on a viaduct overlooking the smoky East End, towering above was the warehouse (located above the goods shed as was the fashion), while down below in the murky brick arches was a vast area for storage of spuds and the like. Burrowing under the lot was a tunnel for suburban traffic to Liverpool Street. Outlying was Spitalfields, an annexe to the main site, used for coal and grain. Although relatively old, having been built in 1881 on the site of Shoreditch, the GER's original passenger terminus, Bishopsgate was well laid out and so had needed few additions.

Aerial view of Bishopsgate goods depot, c.1930: vast swathes of the capital were given over to the goods department. (Author's collection)

As the chief London depot of the Great Eastern, known as the 'Swedey' because of its rural roots, Bishopsgate naturally tended to specialise in incoming agricultural produce. A fair amount of manufactured items arrived from the north via the 'Joint Line', and there was also a flourishing trade in imported goods, especially dairy produce, from the continent via Harwich.

Later developments made little difference to the life of the depot. Unlike other goods termini Bishopsgate did not quietly fade away, but went out in a blaze. On 5 December 1964, practically the whole station was destroyed by fire. The ruins lasted until 2003 when redevelopment began. A new station, Shoreditch High Street, served by the East London line, was opened on the site on 27 April 2010.

Bricklayers Arms

Like Bishopsgate, Bricklayers Arms had started life as a passenger station: the 'Grand West End Terminus' of 1844. However Bricklayers Arms was a contrast to the neat arrangements at the Great Eastern terminus. Here was a hotpot of buildings, mostly brick-dull, squeezed into the site as best as possible. Most interesting was the frontage of the old passenger station, a vast edifice designed by Lewis Cubitt, who also worked on King's Cross. In the midst of the huddle were engine sheds: this juxtaposition was not at all irregular – Camden and King's Cross were similarly laid out. The main entrance, from Old Kent Road, was archetypal – unobtrusive and undistinguished – as were the high surrounding walls. Also typical was the division between inwards and outwards traffic, which was handled in different sheds. A little unusually, Bricklayers Arms included a cattle landing – usually unsanitary livestock was dealt with at a separate site.

Bricklayers Arms goods depot, c.1905: overshadowed by the towering tenements of the Old Kent Road is the main entrance to this depot. (Author's collection)

Bricklayers Arms station, 1844: goods stations often included impressive architectural remains such as this Italianate experiment. (*Illustrated London News*)

Inwards traffic was mostly agricultural produce with manufactured goods outgoing. Although the South Eastern and Chatham Railway had thriving import-export traffic there was no Continental Shed: a separate facility at Ewer Street in Southwark dealt with such items. Mention must also be made of the old London, Chatham and Dover Railway's depot at Blackfriars.

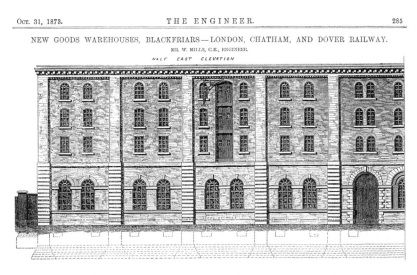

Warehouse, Blackfriars goods depot, 1873: safe storage of goods items was a preoccupation of the railway goods system. (*The Engineer*)

The Southern Railway (SR) brought a certain dynamism to affairs, sensibly uniting Bricklayers Arms with Willow Walk in 1932. Four years later the old passenger station was destroyed by fire. Fire was a perennial hazard for the goods station, with its old buildings and inflammable contents. After heavy damage in the Blitz the depot soldiered on until it closed in 1969. Part continued in use for parcels until 1981. Besides a very nice set of stables in St James Road, there are very few remains today.

Camden

Camden was another higgledy-piggledy stew. Though opened as long ago as 1836 there was almost nothing left from those early years at the turn of the century. The main shed was old (mid-1860s) but nicely arranged. Other buildings included a small wooden shed alongside a dock for goods transhipped to canal. Notable was the invasion of the precincts by the firm of W&A Gilbey, wine and spirit merchants. Gilbey's had a number of rail-served buildings, including 'the Roundhouse', which was built as an engine shed in the 1840s.

Bird's eye view of Camden goods depot, 1896: Camden was a drunkard's paradise, hemmed in and invaded by Gilbey's. (From a contemporary publication)

Camden dealt primarily with manufactured items rather than agricultural produce – the hinterland of the LNWR included the West Midlands and Lancashire. Given the importance of the line it is surprising that Camden was not bigger. However the LNWR had a string of goods facilities in London, including Broad Street, the biggest of the City goods depots, to which Camden was subordinate. Perhaps because of this second-rate status, inwards and outwards traffic was not dealt with in separate buildings, as was common practice elsewhere. Instead, outbound items were dealt with from afternoon to midnight, and then the main shed was turned over to inwards traffic (Bishopsgate had a similar system). The main importance of Camden was as a centre for preliminary marshalling of goods trains, especially those to and from the North London line.

Camden has survived better than almost any other goods depot. Closed in the 1970s, many of the buildings have been adapted for commercial use – including the old stables used for the famous Camden Market.

Commercial Road

The vast bulk of Commercial Road sat like a huge slice of pork pie in the middle of the low-rise Jewish East End. Well designed, if hardly stylish, with a red- and blue-brick industrial appearance, the depot was opened in 1886. It consisted of a high-level 'goods shed' area with platforms for transferring goods to road transport, a storage area in the vaulted space at ground level below, and a four-floor warehouse above.

Shelterers, Commercial Road, 1941: the Tilbury was made (in)famous during the Blitz – the floor was awash with rancid margarine and stale urine. (From a contemporary publication)

The principal trade was in import-export goods for the continent via Tilbury Docks. Indeed the whole of the warehouse was leased out to the dock company and was used for storage of tea, wool and imported food.

The state-owned Port of London Authority took over from the private dock company in 1909, and the Midland ate up the London, Tilbury and Southend Railway in 1912, but these changes of ownership do not seem to have had a great impact on the depot, which remained well used. During the Blitz, Commercial Road became famous as 'The Tilbury' shelter. At the very start of the air-raid period, thousands of East Enders forced their way into the building in the belief that it was a safe haven. Like the tubes it was only relatively so, as the side walls were fairly weak. Fortunately there was no mass disaster (as there could so easily have been) although the roof was mostly destroyed by a direct hit. The depot could not cope with the influx however, and conditions quickly became unsanitary. On the worst nights 14,000 people crammed the vaults and the stink of rancid margarine mixed with faeces and urine was appalling. The depot was closed in the ordinary way in 1967 and was demolished eight years later, apart from the little hydraulic power house which has recently been renovated.

King's Cross

Like a large loaf, King's Cross impressed by its size. Taking up a huge swathe of land, King's Cross was the largest of London's goods depots, but, being reached only by obscure back streets, was still almost unknown. Dominating the site was the huge Granary: six storeys of grimy brick, used, as the name suggests, mainly for storage of grain and flour. Hiding behind it was the inwards shed, like the Granary an older construction dating back to the 1850s. The corresponding outwards shed was an ugly affair of recent vintage. Separating the two sides was an area of viaducts and former coal drops, now mostly converted to warehousing. Coal was the essence of King's Cross goods. Formerly there had been several sets of drops and shoots – in which coal fell down into waiting sacks beneath – but by this time coal was mostly handled at level yards to the north of the site. The most publicly noticeable part of the depot was the rail-served wholesale potato market alongside York Road.

As well as potatoes and coal, King's Cross dealt with all sorts of goods, both manufactured and agricultural – the catchment area of the GNR was spread wide across the Midlands and north, passing up into Scotland via connecting lines.

There was little later development at King's Cross. The London and North Eastern Railway (LNER) was the worst off of all the interwar companies and consequently could do little to develop its facilities. Closure was pretty protracted: general goods went in 1973, although a replacement modern depot stayed in occasional use until 1987. Some of the sidings to the north remained in use until the current redevelopment programme began. There are considerable relics, including the Granary.

THE GREAT NORTHERN RAILWAY.

Warehouse, King's Cross goods depot, 1853: like several other depots, King's Cross featured transhipment facilities to water transport. (*Illustrated London News*)

Marylebone

Marylebone was the immaculate soufflé of London's goods stations. Only recently completed, it had a fine range of well-designed buildings, spaciously laid out in the best fan pattern layout. Here was the red-brick goods shed with warehouse above: it was one of the largest of its type in the capital. There was also an ample coal yard, segregated from the rest of the depot in the correct fashion to avoid dust and fuss. Forming the frontage was a range of red-brick offices. Not far off was the railway's own power station (all but obligatory in those pre-mains days). And by the canal was a wharf with a handsomely curved canopy for goods destined for watery places. Altogether the depot was the best designed in London. Unfortunately, like the passenger station, it was the least busy.

Traffic was a mixed bag of industrial and agricultural products, with the former perhaps predominant. One of the most important items handled was fish from Grimsby. Fish and milk were handled at a short landing with its own approach east of the main line. This arrangement, which was quite common at contemporary goods depots, ensured speedy despatch of perishable goods – essential before refrigeration came into use.

Marylebone had a sad fate. The warehouse was destroyed by bombing during the war and was not rebuilt. The rest of the depot continued in (under) use until closure in 1966. The site has been used for housing.

Nine Elms

Nine Elms was the busiest of the goods depots south of the Thames and was a queer mixture of efficiency and muddle. The two main sheds were quite businesslike, being spacious and well laid out. The Old Shed, for inwards and import-export traffic, incorporated the wooden roofed shed and booking office building of the earlier passenger station of 1838–48 (the forerunner of Waterloo). Unusually in the workaday world of the goods depot, the latter was of some architectural style. The New Shed, just a year old, dealt with most of the outbound goods. The muddle came with the complex of yards, wharves and scabby old buildings north of Nine Elms Lane. This was linked to the main site via level crossings over which every wagon had to pulled by horse preceded by a man with a red flag or lamp. Doubtless this inconvenience was the aspect of the depot that impinged on the public perception. Adjacent to the northern site was the elegant eighteenth-century mansion known as Brunswick House on Wandsworth Road, which functioned as a social club for the depot's workers.

As with the other southern depots, agricultural produce in and manufactured goods out was the main pattern. The most important specialist traffic was imports and exports to and from the Continent and elsewhere via the railway-owned Southampton Docks.

The depot was greatly expanded in Edwardian times by the addition of the old locomotive works, which became Nine Elms South. The Southern Railway era saw the redevelopment of the wharf area, with a huge new warehouse, as well as wholesale alterations to the southern annexe. Closure came in 1968. The majority of the site is now taken up by the new Covent Garden Market but one block of the old works and Brunswick House (today looking very forlorn) survives.

The yard, Paddington goods depot, c.1920: at the turn of the century, this was perhaps the most chaotic of the depots. (Author's collection)

Paddington

As with Bishopsgate and Marylebone, Paddington goods had been built all at once. However, unlike those two, by 1900 it was a bit of a dog's dinner. Partly this was the fault of Brunel's original design of the 1850s, which in contrast to the simple and elegant layout of the passenger station, was convoluted and sprawling. The ugly metal viaduct running through the main shed to the high-level coal yard by the Grand Union was not so much the problem as the narrow wooden platforms with lack of adequate cartage access. Partly it was historical. The main sheds with glazed roofs were still in good repair for their age, but the original warehouse had been burnt down some fifteen years earlier and was never rebuilt. The replacement storage facilities were ad hoc. Overall the place was shabby and ramshackle.

The goods shed, Paddington goods depot, 1929: after the rebuilding, Paddington was a model of order and efficiency. (Author's collection)

Traffic was heavy. Mainly this was manufactured items outbound, with fruit and vegetables inbound, although paper from South Wales, West Midlands manufactures and other items also featured in the latter. Heavier items and bulk goods were handled at Westbourne Park, there being no yard to speak of at Paddington itself.

In 1925 the Great Western began to redevelop the station. With a new shed, clear of clutter, the new depot was the most modern in London and the only one built for motor vehicles. Closure came in 1975. The buildings were demolished a decade later. The only relic is the former Mint Stables, now in use as part of a hospital.

St Pancras

St Pancras came in two parts. To the north was St Pancras goods station proper, also known as Agar Town. This dealt primarily with incoming goods. Its big beefy shed was relatively old, dating back to the 1860s, but like everything Midland was ship-shape and business-like. Glued to the south side of the goods shed was an arched span, a miniature version of Barlow's roof at St Pancras, which provided shelter for the depot's blossoming collection of motor vehicles. The Agar Town site also had extensive yards, especially for serving coal traffic, but including the pride of the depot – an early gantry crane. These powerful beasts would later find a key role dealing with container traffic. There was also a large warehouse – inventively known as the Granary. Somers Town, the outwards half of the depot, fronted Euston Road. Although a gem amongst goods stations, it looked dowdy

In the subterranean track, St Pancras goods station, 1899: in contrast to the nobility of the passenger station, goods facilities were decidedly grim. (From a contemporary journal)

by the side of the soaring spires of the sainted passenger station. Somers Town had a split-level arrangement. The main goods shed and warehouse – separate buildings here – were at viaduct height, with a wholesale fruit and vegetable market below. To the back of Somers Town was Purchese Street coal depot, which was the biggest of its type in London. Flanking the main line were two further coal yards.

From all this mention of the c-word it is obvious what one of the most important concerns of the depot was. There was also a thriving trade in manufactured goods, both inwards and outwards, as well as vegetables and fruit. A specialisation was in beer from Burton, Britain's brewing town. The huge kegs of this were once stored beneath the passenger station, a rare intrusion of goods into the passenger world.

Apart from damage during the Blitz, there was little change in the depot until closure in the late 1960s. The new British Library has been built on the Somers Town site, while Agar Town is mostly used for housing. A few traces of the old depot remain, including the old power station which is used as a youth sports club.

Willow Walk

Willow Walk was the smaller, Brighton side of Bricklayers Arms. The situation was much the same as at London Bridge or Victoria: two companies occupying adjacent but separate sites, with a 'Chinese wall' down the middle. The depot was physically much the same as Bricklayers Arms – a ragout of Victorian buildings – but of less intrinsic interest as this site had never been used for passengers.

The kind of traffic was also similar to Bricklayers Arms – manufactured goods out and agricultural produce in. Here, however, import-export traffic was prominent.

Willow Walk was very much the odd man out of the line up of 1900 as it was soon to vanish, being incorporated into Bricklayers Arms. Several of its buildings disappeared in the amalgamation of 1932 or during the Blitz, and certainly it lost any vestige of a separate existence. The remaining buildings were demolished during redevelopment in the mid-1980s.

Annexe: That's Not My Name

Bricklayers Arms, Nine Elms, King's Cross: romantic names for unromantic places. The naming of stations conforms to certain patterns. In London this is geographic: streets, areas or some prominent feature. Of the termini, nine were originally street names, three were districts and two were landmarks. Both the crosses were road intersections, the monuments being long gone. Victoria was a special case: Victoria Street seems to have given the area its informal regal title which was then transferred to the station. Bricklayers Arms, unusually, was named after a coaching inn. What is seldom appreciated is how rare this pattern is.

Elsewhere in Britain, stations tended towards geographical titles – but only tended. Non-geographical names included 'Victoria', which was a firm favourite all over, with 'Exchange' and 'Central' big in the north. The latter was as much boosting the Great Central company as it was a indicator of centrality. Leeds had a 'New', which, by the time it was renamed in the 1930s, was actually quite old. Perhaps most fanciful is Edinburgh's Waverley, derived from Walter Scott's romantic novels.

Originally the names of the big London stations took after their owning company: thus Euston was the North Western terminus. The switch to geographically based titles occurred in the 1860s, with the proliferation of termini. The continent generally followed the old London pattern. This was particularly true in Berlin and Vienna. The latter had a full set of compass points, roughly indicating their location in the city as well as the districts of the old empire that they served. Their origin however, was strictly commercial. The situation in Paris was a little different. There, as in London, termini began to breed. Thus the old Ouest became Montparnasse to distinguish it from the Ouest's other station, Saint-Lazare. Austerlitz/Orleans was stuck halfway for the best part of a century.

In Russia, stations were named for locations reached from them. This practice probably had commercial origins but later became geographical. Surprisingly, little effort was made to give station names a red tinge (the Moscow Metro, on the other hand, was awash). In fact, the reverse is true – in Moscow, Tsarist

Bombay Victoria station, c.1905: the name of this Asian masterpiece has proved contentious in recent years. (Author's collection)

Alexsandrovsky and Nikolayevsky got the boot, and were replaced by apolitical geographical terms.

In contrast, Eire went in for political re-education in a big way. In 1966, fifteen stations across the nation were renamed after heroes of the Easter Rebellion. Ireland was no stranger to such retitlings. After the eviction of the English oppressors, royalist Queenstown and Kingstown became Cobh and Dún Laoghaire respectively.

There is no particular pattern in America. Chicago can be taken as typical, although each city had its peculiarities. Two of its stations took after streets, two after companies and two were descriptive – Union and Grand Central. The latter very much expresses the modesty and tact of the inhabitants of the Grand Republic.

Only in places deeply associated with Britain, such as Argentina and India, does the geographical predominate – an enduring legacy of the first railway nation. An exception in the latter is the subcontinent's most beautiful station, Mumbai Chhatrapathi Shivaji Terminus (formerly Bombay Victoria).

1910: A TRAVELLER CAME BY, SILENTLY, INVISIBLY

London's First Tubes

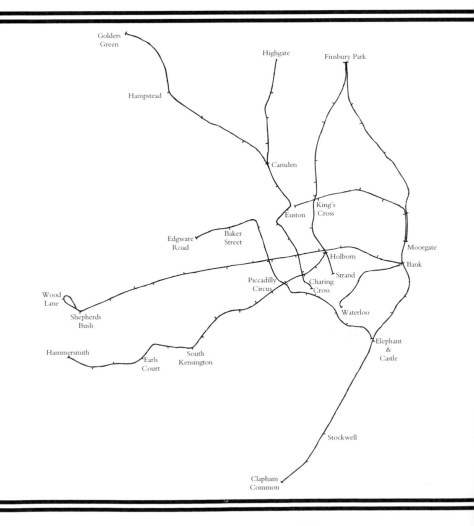

London's tube railways in 1910.

'The Tube' is currently a generic term for all London's underground railways. Originally, it was applied solely to the entirely electric, deep-level lines using metal-lined circular cross-section tunnels.

Deep Level Underground Electric Railways, 1910

Railway	Length	Stations	Colour*
Waterloo & City	1m 36ch	2	grey
Great Northern & City	3m 39ch	6	orange
Baker Street & Waterloo	4m 27ch	11	brown
Central London	6m 69ch	14	blue
City & South London	7m 21ch	15	dark grey
Charing Cross, Euston & Hampstead	7m 71ch	16	light grey
Great Northern, Piccadilly & Brompton	7m 38ch	22	yellow

Railways were traditionally measured in chains and miles: 80 chains (ch) = 1 mile (m).

The colours used for the lines on contemporary maps varied – these are the best fit possible (the Metropolitan and District were red and green respectively).

The tube railways were built as commercial undertakings, not for the convenience of Londoners. Limited early success went sour and, by 1910, the tubes barely turned a profit. Despite extension and amalgamation, the tubes became state property in 1933 – the fate of all losers. As well as being a market failure, the tubes were also a failure of the market. When local capital sensibly shunned the loss-making new railways, foreign finance, reckless and ill-informed, stepped in. From a business perspective, the Yerkes tubes (Piccadilly, Hampstead, Bakerloo) shouldn't have been built.

Urban transport in other places and at other times produced some of the world's best architecture. This cannot be said of the tubes. The domed buildings of the City and South London (C&SL) had some merit, and aficionados may find a primitive charm on the Great Northern and City (GN&C). The Yerkes lines' buildings, however, were dreadful: the overall impact clumsy, the colouring grotesque, the detailing feeble, the tiling inferior to the average suburban butcher's shop. Leslie Green's vast output is an enduring blot on the London landscape.

The gated end platform was characteristic of the early tube rolling stock. This was quickly outdated technology, contributing much to the early withdrawal of the vast fleet of the Yerkes tubes. The lightly built cars were also not fit for lengthy outdoor runs on the interwar extensions. In some cases, lifespan was little more than twenty years. Compare this with, say, the 1938 tube stock, which remains in service today.

The engineering of the tubes was entirely up to scratch, the construction efficient, and the electrical systems innovatory, if uncoordinated. The execution,

A visit to the works, *c.*1895: the technology which made it all possible, the Greathead Shield. (*The Graphic*)

however, left much to be desired. For legal reasons all lines followed surface roads (resulting in extreme curvature), stations were placed far too frequently, and junctions in the central area were installed. The legacy of the early lack of planning on the current London Underground in terms of speed and reliability of service has been, quite simply, disastrous.

Waterloo and City Railway

The Waterloo and City (W&C) was one of the earliest tube railways and one of the oddest. Traditionally it formed part of the national railway system rather than being one of London's own, and has remained an isolated shuttle service all its life.

'The Drain', probably named for its unpleasant demeanour, opened on 8 August 1898 and was the culmination of sixty years of attempts to reach the City by the

Waterloo station, c.1900: dark and dingy down below, it was known as 'The Drain'. (Author's collection)

Waterloo and City Railway train, c.1900: American styling was all the rage on the tube – this looks like it has a cowcatcher!

London and South Western Railway. At Waterloo commuters descended into the arches below the main line and, after a short journey, emerged at the Bank intersection. There were no surface buildings – a rarity amongst the early tubes. The main service was provided by four five-car trains built by Jackson and Sharp of Wilmington, Delaware. A pair of singletons by Dick, Kerr of Preston was used off-peak. All stock featured gated ends that were manually operated by guards, as was current practice. Electrification was at 530v d.c.; distribution by central conductor rail. Power was provided by a power station at Waterloo, coal for which was brought down to the tunnel and moved along by a small service locomotive, then hoisted up again. A small depot was also located here.

The original stock was replaced in 1940, when the line adopted the Southern Railway standard electric system. There were no survivors, although the cute little shunting loco, withdrawn in 1968, is preserved at the National Railway Museum. Since 1994, the Waterloo and City has been an integral part of London Underground.

Great Northern and City Railway

The Great Northern and City was the only tube built to take full-size rolling stock, although in the event the line remained a simple Finsbury Park–Moorgate trek for some seventy years.

The original purpose of the GN&C was to allow Great Northern Railway suburban services to run through to the City. Exchange to electric loco haulage was to be made at Finsbury Park high level, before passing underground at Drayton Park, not far south. However, the GNR got cold feet and withdrew, building a separate underground terminus at Finsbury Park instead. Tunnels were still constructed full-size and the electric system allowed clearance for main-line stock (conductor rails outside the running rails) in the hope that the GNR would see

Essex Road station, c.1905: the architecture wasn't up to much but then there wasn't a lot in the way of intermediate traffic. (Author's collection)

Great Northern & City Railway train, c.1905: big rattan-covered seats, wide windows, but not going anywhere worth seeing. (Author's collection)

the light. Opening was on 14 February 1904 – St Valentine's Day – but there was nothing lovely here. The multiple-unit cars were by Brush Electrical Engineering of Loughborough. The fifty-eight originals made extensive use of mahogany and teak, with eighteen steel-panelled cars added in 1906. Access was by central sliding door, operated by platform staff, and by gates at the ends. Six-car formations were operated, reduced to two cars off peak. The depot was at Drayton Park. Power, at 575v d.c., was generated at Poole Street, Shoreditch.

The GN&C became part of the Metropolitan in 1913. The power station was then shut down, becoming the famous Gainsborough film studios, and first class was introduced – this was the only tube catering for the nobs. The line passed to London Transport with the Metropolitan in 1933, shortly thereafter becoming part of the Northern Line. Tube stock and the conventional four-rail system were introduced. The line remained self-contained however, until it was transferred to British Railways as part of the Great Northern Electrics in 1976.

Baker Street and Waterloo Railway

The Baker Street and Waterloo Railway (BS&W), by this time already commonly known as the Bakerloo line, was the archetypal tube railway. Together with the Piccadilly and Hampstead lines, it formed the core of the London Underground system.

The line ought to have been called the Waterloo and West End Railway – Baker Street was more a convenient end than a proper beginning. There had long been

Baker Street station, 1906: a typical station by Leslie Green, this example has been demolished. (Author's collection)

plans for this route and the proposal of 1892 seemed likely to join its pipedream predecessors. Fortunately, a backer, the London and Globe, was found and construction started in 1898. It finished two years later when the London and Globe collapsed ignominiously. The BS&W found an unsavoury saviour in Charles Tyson Yerkes, whose group bought up the unfinished works in 1902. An able organiser, Yerkes was also a convicted felon, blackmailer and dispenser of big bungs. Yankee verve soon got things moving, with the first section opening on 10 March 1906. By 1910, the line extended from the Elephant to Edgware Road. Station buildings were by Leslie Green. Unattractive things they were, of maroon glazed terracotta, unredeemed by feeble art nouveau touches. The American Car and Foundry Company provided 108 cars. The depot was in London Road near Waterloo. Power came from the District's Lots Road.

The Bakerloo forged what was to be a pattern of extending out of the central area, to Watford by 1917. The primeval stock was junked not long after. The line remains one of the least altered of the tubes, even retaining its original southern terminus.

Central London Railway

The Central London Railway (CLR) was different from the lines covered so far, in that it was purely an urban transport system with no interchange with existing conventional railways.

Shepherds Bush station, *c.*1905: a popular view – as well as serving the locals, this was also where tram passengers from the far west went underground. (Author's collection)

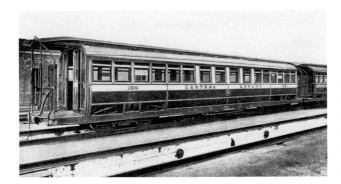

Central London Railway car, *c.*1905: each end was provided with a man to open the doors, which was very labour-intensive work. (Author's collection)

Plans for the line were formulated early on. The route was an obvious one – along the spine of London from the inner western suburbs through the West End to the City. The line seemed a good prospect and financial backing was soon found. The CLR was ceremonially opened on 27 June 1900 by the Prince of Wales (soon to be King Edward VII), with public use beginning on 30 July. Stations, inoffensive affairs with beige terracotta facings, were the work of Harry Measures. The line was originally worked by locomotives, twenty-eight being supplied by General Electric of Schnectady in the Empire State. The 168 carriages, of the gated sort, were made at the Ashbury works in Manchester. But the locos caused unacceptable vibration and so, in 1903, sixty-four multiple unit style driving motors were acquired. The depot and power station were at Wood Lane, to which a passenger service was commenced in 1908 to serve the White City exhibition. The 550v d.c. central conducting rail system was used. The CLR was initially very popular, and seized public imagination, becoming known as the Twopenny ('tuppenny') Tube from the flat fare, which was dropped in 1907.

The CLR passed to the Underground Group in 1913, which abolished its non-standard features between the wars. With post-war extensions to the far east and west, the Central became the longest Underground line. An interesting survivor is ESL107, a service locomotive made from the head ends of two 1903 motors. This remained in use into the '90s and is now preserved at London Transport Museum's Acton Depot.

City and South London Railway

The City and South London Railway was the first underground electric railway in the world. Its general methods were later universal but its details were quite unique.

The project started life as the City of London and Southwark Subway. The idea came from the Tower Subway of 1870, which the company's engineer, James Henry Greathead, had helped to build. The new line was to be short, cable worked, with small tunnels constructed by shield. Supply difficulties and practical doubts opened the way for electricity. Renaming to the City and South London Railway occurred shortly before the first section, City to Stockwell, opened on

Stockwell station, c.1905: a fine dome and classical styling but the fruit shop was more important to Daisy, the sender of this postcard. (Author's collection)

City & South London Railway train, c.1905: the man on the right needn't look so C&A casual – driving a mine engine is nothing to be proud of. (Author's collection)

18 December 1890. By 1910, the C&SLR extended from Euston to Clapham Common. Unusually, several stations had island platforms. Surface buildings, quiet and refined, mostly in red brick with white-stone classical details, were by T. Phillips Figgis. If not well known, Figgis was a recognised architect, which was uncommon for those working on the tubes. Also unlike other tubes, the C&SL was always locomotive-worked. The locos, ultimately fifty-two in number, were tiny, British-made (!) four-wheelers. The carriages, known facetiously as padded cells, operated in three, later four, rake trains. The depot at Stockwell was accessed by cable-worked incline, a relic of the original scheme. Electricity at 500v d.c. was generated at Stockwell – the inspiration for H.G. Wells' appallingly racist short story *The Lord of the Dynamos*. Pick up was third rail, off-set between the rails.

The C&SL was taken by the Underground Group in 1913. Stockwell power station closed shortly thereafter and plans were made to extend to Morden and integrate with Hampstead. This was not completed until 1926. The combined line became the Northern in 1937. The domed station at Kennington survives, as does the head office at Moorgate. The London Transport Museum houses a locomotive and a carriage.

Charing Cross, Euston and Hampstead Railway

The Charing Cross, Euston and Hampstead Railway (CCE&HR), shortened to Hampstead Tube in contemporary usage, was the other half of what was to be the

Golders Green station, c.1910: the plain brick must have been a bit of a relief for Green after all that maroon tiling. (Author's collection)

Northern Line. This was the most standardised of the tube railways but still had several interesting features.

The CCE&HR opened for the public on 23 June 1907. Known as the 'Last Link', it consisted of a Charing Cross to Golders Green main line with a branch to Highgate (now Archway). The line had been authorised in the wake of the C&SL in the early 1990s, but not started. This was the first to be snatched up by Yerkes but the last to be built. It featured similar stations to the Bakerloo and Piccadilly, used the same type of rolling stock – 150 cars made by the American Car and Foundry Co. – and drew electricity from the same source. However, the line was the only early tube with a regularly used junction – at Camden. Golders Green was the first of the underground suburbs; here also was the depot. Interestingly, North End (Bull and Bush) was an unopened station, complete at platform level but not connected to the surface.

Extended north to Edgware and south to join the City and South London at Kennington, the Hampstead was the first tube to lose its original rolling stock (1929). Long ago swallowed up by the slovenly nightmare that is the Northern Line, the Hampstead is the most vanished of the old tubes.

Great Northern, Piccadilly and Brompton Railway

The Great Northern, Piccadilly and Brompton (GNP&B), or Piccadilly for short, was the third of the Yerkes tubes. Like the others, it was highly standardised but had features of note.

The GNP&B was a conflation of two pre-existing schemes: the Great Northern and Strand (the West End equivalent of the Great Northern and City) and the Brompton and Piccadilly Circus, which would have connected to the District at South Kensington. Neither got off the drawing board. Yerkes purchased the rights in 1901. Connecting the two at Holborn, a western extension to Hammersmith was added. The line was quickly built and opened on 15 December 1906. A branch to the Strand (later Aldwych), a vestige of the original Great Northern and Strand plan, followed a year later. Characteristic were the closely spaced stations of standard Yerkes design. Rolling stock was also of the common type, although here the 218 cars were mainly acquired from continental sources (France and Hungary). The depot was at Lillie Bridge, north of Earls Court. The most interesting location on the line is South Kensington. This station was laid out for cross platform interchange with the projected express District line (if only). The corresponding platforms were constructed and fully fitted out but never used.

Above: Motor car, Great Northern, Piccadilly & Brompton Railway, c.1906: tube trains still had a separate engine compartment up until the 1930s. (Author's collection)

Right: Interior of car, Great Northern, Piccadilly & Brompton Railway, c.1906: the interior of an early tube train was function not decorative. (Author's collection)

The Piccadilly is perhaps the most changed of all the tube lines. Its inner-city stations were mostly rebuilt between the wars, and in 1932–3 the line was extended west to Hounslow and Uxbridge and north to Cockfosters. By this time the original gate stock was gone, except on the Aldwych branch where, rebuilt for shuttle use, it lingered until 1949. The Aldwych branch is a rare example of a closed tube line. This ghost station allegedly has its own ghost, which, like the well-known William Terriss who appears at Covent Garden, comes from the acting fraternity. Although not used for passengers since 1994, it is familiar from its use as a film location and as such preserves the essence of the old Great Northern, Piccadilly and Brompton Railway.

Annexe: Going Underground

Architecture on the early London Underground was at its best undistinguished. And at its worst appalling: there are few buildings anywhere, railway or no, as vile as Leslie Green's maroon horrors. What a contrast there was elsewhere.

Hector Guimard's entrances for the Paris Metro (1900–12) are probably the finest works of 'Underground art'. Although only young, Guimard was already an accomplished architect. A standardised kit with interchangeable parts to fit any site was provided. Central was the green cast-iron shield marked with a letter 'M' for Métropolitain surrounded by the flowing lines of the art nouveau. Other elements included a sturdy stone base, etiolated lamp brackets, and, on the larger examples, nicknamed *libellules* (dragonflies) by Parisians, enamelled panels and glass roofs. Originally 141 of all types were built – eighty or so remain in situ. Working examples can be found at Montreal, Mexico City, Chicago and Lisbon, with art displays at Toledo and MOMA. The *édicules* (kiosks) have superb detailing, have proved hard-wearing, and, because of standardisation, were cheap. These Parisian wonders are typical of the thought put into the Metro and are a real credit to the city.

The Vienna Stadtbahn (1898–1901), on the other hand, was a work of art. Otto Wagner's designs were comprehensive, encompassing not only station architecture, but also works of engineering and furnishings right down to door handles. The total artwork even extended to the carriages of the trains. Wagner was an artistic genius, the greatest architect ever to be let loose on the railways of a national capital, and a leading light of the Vienna Secession. On the earlier lines, a free interpretation of classical forms dominated – the acme being reached with the baroque Hofpavilion at Hietzing. Later on, art nouveau ran riot. The Karlplatz station, with its magnificent golden sunflower decorations, is the showpiece of this phase and is one of the most photographed stations in the world. All was white and bright and clean. And powered by steam! Like the Austrian Empire itself, the Imperial capital's urban transport system was old wine in new bottles.

Bastille station, Paris, c.1910: biggest of the kiosks, the styling is just plain weird. (Author's collection)

Oberbaumbruecke, Berlin, c.1903: medieval looks + electricity = Kaiserzeit. (Author's collection)

This was a magnificent work of art, an ideological boost for the monarchy, but it was also a really bad railway – noisy, dirty and slow.

The foregoing examples are, perhaps, a little unfair; Paris and Vienna were and are something akin to open-air museums. Look, then, at huge, sprawling, gritty Berlin, the continental city most London-ish. Here, the U-Bahn threw up an astounding range of architecture, historical and modernist. The first line

(1902), being mostly elevated, provided the most prominent examples, with traditional German forms tending to predominate. Outstanding was Otto Stahn's Oberbaumbrücke, carried out in north German brick, gothic and resembling an old city gate. Elsewhere, there were art nouveau traces and unclassifiable but undoubtedly modern touches. Unlike Paris or Vienna, this was a group effort, although one of the workers, the Swede Alfred Grenander, went on to become the house architect. Despite war, division and modernisation, there is still a lot to see in this quirky but ultra-efficient urban railway.

In terms of architectural influence, that of the early London tubes was approximately zero. And rightly so. The Paris Metro, an open-air art gallery; Vienna's Stadtbahn, an imperial showpiece; and the Berlin U-Bahn, showcase for individual architects, were, however, precursors of the greatest of all underground railways, the Moscow Metro.

London's Suburban Electrics

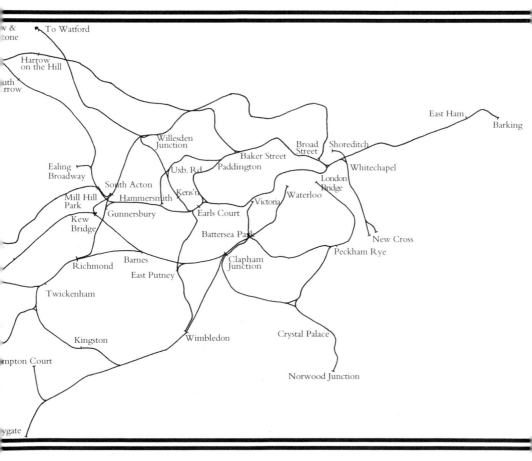

Electrified lines in 1920.

The first two decades of the twentieth century were rife with electrification schemes. By 1920 six had been completed in the London area:

Suburban Electrification Projects, 1920

Railway	Year	Miles	Type of electrification (power supply)
District	1903	43	fourth rail, 600v d.c. (Lots Road PS)
Metropolitan	1905	29	fourth rail, 600v d.c. (Neasden PS)
H&C	1906	5	fourth rail, 600v d.c. (Park Royal PS)
LBSCR	1909	25	overhead, 6700v a.c. (mains)
LNWR	1914	30	fourth rail, 630v d.c. (Stonebridge Park PS)
LSWR	1915	50	third rail, 630v d.c. (Durnsford Road PS)

There were, ostensibly, a variety of reasons for electrification – but the bottom line was financial. Most suburban railways were losing revenue due to competition from tubes and trams. Electric trains were seen as being able to stem this loss. They were cheaper to run, being more efficient in their use of fuel than steam (as already outlined in the 1850 section), and with faster acceleration they could speed service and increase capacity. However, electrification had high start-up costs – the possible gain would have to justify the expenditure – and was, therefore, suitable for only heavily used lines.

Steam and electric side by side at Edgware Road, c.1905: in with the new. (Author's collection)

Locomotives being scrapped at Neasden, c.1910: out with the old. (Author's collection)

Initially the type of system used – overhead high voltage alternating current, or low voltage conductor rail direct current – was fairly arbitrary, with the line being electrified defining the method chosen (overhead being unsuitable for tunnel working for example). As in the matter of gauge, the pioneer seemed to have the edge; the pioneer in this case being the conductor rail system. Virtually all early electrifications in the capital eventually used a system compatible with this. Initially, this was of no particular relevance, however later developments saw the system spread across the south – on main lines where it was not suitable for fast running.

The results of electrification were varied. The District electrification instantly boosted the carrying capacity of the line: for instance, on the South Kensington to Mansion House stretch the number of trains each way per day increased from 269 in 1904 to 478 in 1905. This did not mean vastly increased numbers of passengers, which had to wait for the spread of suburban development that eventually swamped the District. As a result the Hounslow and Uxbridge services were transferred to Piccadilly in the 1930s. On the South London line, on the other hand, the increase in the number of passengers was initially large – a 63 per cent gain for two months, December 1909 and January 1910 – but in the long term the decrease in the line's usage was probably only staved off and today it is a decided backwater.

In fact, most of the increase in speed and capacity was a result of signalling and other tweaks – the Great Eastern's steam-powered jazz alternative resulted in similar gains. The true gain was in cost – electric was far cheaper – but there were also gains in comfort and image, which were vital in the coming consumer age.

District

The inadequacies of steam traction in the tunnelled portions of the Metropolitan and District railways had always been recognised. Yet there was nothing else available. By the late 1890s the feasibility of electric working had been demonstrated and the two companies joined forces for electrification trials. This cooperation was forced upon the two railways, rivals elsewhere, by the Inner Circle service (see 1880 section) which ran over portions of both railways. The fruit of the joint effort culminated in late 1900, when track between Earls Court and High Street Kensington was electrified, and a 'novelty' passenger service provided. At the end of 1901 a decision was made to electrify the Inner Circle on a four-rail, 600v d.c. system.

A start was made on the new Ealing and South Harrow line. This 5-mile branch was adopted as a further testing ground, particularly for track circuiting and automatic signalling. Two seven-car trains were delivered to work the line in March 1903. These were American in style with boarded wooden exteriors, clerestory roofs and arched windows. At first these were painted eggnog yellow, a bizarre sight in this still-rural area. In American fashion they were known as 'cars' – a term standard on the Underground ever since. The line was opened on 23 June 1903 from Mill Hill Park (now Acton Town) to Park Royal for exhibition traffic, and throughout four days later.

District train at Ealing Broadway, *c.*1910: early electric trains tended towards boxiness. (Author's collection)

The rest of the District was electrified in 1905, starting with the South Acton-Hounslow shuttle on 13 June 1905. The rest followed, with the last District steamer running on 5 November. Steam did not die away entirely: Midland goods trains to depots in Kensington, running via the Super Circle route, continued into the 1960s.

Multiple units provided most of the services. Later called B stock, these numbered 420 cars. The new trains had the Underground's first air-operated doors, although these did not work well and were shortly removed. Works and car sheds were provided at Mill Hill Park. The District also bought ten boxy little electric locos for hauling LNWR Outer Circle trains from Earls Court to Mansion House.

Electric for the District came from the huge power station at Lots Road, Chelsea, which was said to be biggest in the world at the time. Located on the Thames near the West London Extension Railway, Lots Road had a capacity of 44,000kW and supplied most of the tube railways as well as the District.

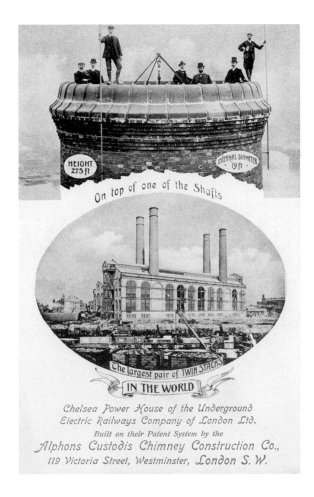

Lots Road Power Station, c.1905: the builders were obviously very proud of their achievement, as well they might be. (Author's collection)

The District electrification was perhaps the most successful of all and results soon started to show. Electrification proved a turning point in the District's fortune and to reflect this many of the stations, which had often previously been temporary-looking gimcrack affairs, were soon rebuilt to the designs of H.W. Ford.

The initial electric stock had a surprisingly short life with the South Harrow cars being scrapped in 1925. The main stock lasted a decade or so longer. The locomotives went at around the same time, having found use on an Ealing Broadway to Southend service (with the change to steam at Barking) after the Outer Circle was clipped at the end of 1908. The final survivor of the District electrification was Lots Road, which was closed in 2001 and is being converted to housing.

Metropolitan

The Metropolitan Railway was a much larger concern than the District, stretching out into rural Oxfordshire and Buckinghamshire. Only the urban and suburban sections were considered as candidates for electrification, which of necessity had to match that of the District. The Baker Street to Harrow section of the main line and the new Uxbridge branch were selected, in addition to the northern half of the Inner Circle.

The electrics were formally inaugurated on New Year's Day 1905, when the General Manager was presented with a silver motorman's key with which he drove the first public train from Uxbridge to Baker Street. By the end of March, all Uxbridge services were electric. Steam haulage into Baker Street continued

Metropolitan electric train, c.1905: the 'Met' electrics were more stylish than the District's and came with go-faster stripes. (Author's collection)

until 1 November 1906 when electric locomotives began to haul main-line trains operating south of Wembley. The interchange point was switched to Harrow in 1908.

The Circle line was next, with electrics commencing on 1 July 1905. However, it was found that Metropolitan collecting gear caused damage to District rails and the service was immediately withdrawn except for an Aldgate-South Kensington shuttle. A limited service recommenced on 3 September, with the full electric coming on 24 September. The last steam hauled passenger trains over the Circle were the Great Western suburban services, which became loco-hauled on 2 September 1907. Steam survived on goods, working to the Great Western's Smithfield depot until 1960.

As an adjunct, electrification was extended to the East London on 31 March 1913, with a full service of electric trains both local and through.

To run the services the Metropolitan ordered 234 cars. These were similar to those of the District but had gated ends (later converted to closed vestibules) and no centre doors. The new stock was emblazoned with a coat of arms which proclaimed *Vis Vincta Servii* – strength subdued serves. Unlike the District, which scrapped all existing stock, the Met converted some carriages for electric running. The Metropolitan had a number of electric locomotives: ten each of British Westinghouse camelbacks (known as 'Bovril Bottles') and boxy British Thomson Houstons. As well as forwarding suburban services, the locos worked the Metropolitan's goods station in Clerkenwell, which was reputedly the first entirely electrically worked goods depot in the world.

Power was generated at Neasden, where the works and car sheds were also located. The power station, with an ornamental red-brick façade, had an output of 10,500kW.

The electrification was not accompanied by a major station rebuilding programme. The characteristic white tiled edifices and the great pile at Baker Street had to wait until the 1920s.

Neasden Power Station, *c*.1905: looking more like a mill – in the background is 'Watkin's Folly', the would-be Eiffel Tower at Wembley. (Author's collection)

NEASDEN POWER STATION.

The electrification was very successful. There were two further extensions – beyond Harrow to Watford and Rickmansworth in 1925 and to Amersham and Chesham in 1961. The early electric stock was withdrawn by the time of the Second World War. The locomotives proved to be unsatisfactory and were replaced in 1921–3 by twenty Metropolitan-Vickers engines. Neasden power station closed on 21 July 1968 and the chimneys were blown up in the autumn of the following year.

Hammersmith and City

Of the early electric schemes, the Paddington to Hammersmith was the least known as the line was usually regarded as a branch of the Metropolitan. Though the conversion was carried out by the Great Western Railway the system chosen was identical to that on the Inner Circle due to the necessity of through running.

Electric traction started on 5 November 1906 with a Hammersmith to Aldgate routing. Steam could still be found on the GWR's Aldgate-Richmond service. This was soon cut back to a Notting Hill-Richmond shuttle and ceased at the end of 1910.

Twenty six-car trains, much like those on the Metropolitan, were purchased. Although lettered as if jointly owned, cars belonged either to the GWR or Metropolitan. Power was supplied by the Great Western's Park Royal generating station, which had an output of 6,000kW. Park Royal also served the GWR's own needs and later provided power for the Central Line's White City-Ealing

Hammersmith station, c.1910: as rebuilt for the electrification. (Author's collection)

Broadway section. As with the District, the opportunity was taken to rebuild several stations and generally tidy up the line.

H&C services took much of their current form at the start of the Second World War, when the link to Kensington was also taken out of action. The joint stock was withdrawn at this time. After a period of storage, some cars were sent to Merseyside, while others found use as dormitories for Bevin Boys and sailors. Park Royal Power Station closed in 1936, although the main-line company and its successors continued to supply power for the H&C until the 1970s.

South London Line

While earlier projects were complete in themselves, the South London electrification was part of a much bigger scheme. The LBSCR adopted the high-voltage overhead alternating current system, which was held to be more suitable for long-distance use, with an eye to converting its main line, testing the waters on the South London.

The 'Elevated Electric' commenced running from London Bridge to Victoria on 1 December 1909. Extensions followed to Crystal Palace and Norwood Junction on 12 May 1911, and from Streatham Hill to Peckham Rye on 1 March 1912. Unlike earlier schemes, steam services continued to use the electrified lines.

Eight three-car trains, made up of first-class trailers sandwiched by third-class motors, were initially provided. Liveried in umber and cream, the vehicles were

Overhead wires at Peckham Rye station, c.1910: the overhead was visually intrusive but highly efficient. (Author's collection)

Overhead electric train, c.1925: this train is from the last batch of overhead stock, built for Coulsdon services. (Lens of Sutton)

boxy affairs with semi-open compartments and side gangways. The stock was well appointed and gave an excellent performance. Electric locomotives were built for the extended services. To lower costs a separate power station was not built; juice was taken instead from the mains of the London Electric Supply Corporation at Denmark Hill.

After the Great War, the Southern overheaded to Coulsdon and Sutton but then decided to concentrate its resources on third rail. The overhead lines were converted to third rail in 1928–9. The South London stock was converted to third rail operation, the carriages found a home on the Wimbledon–West Croydon line whilst the motors were eventually returned to their original home. Both continued in use into the 1950s.

London and North Western

The London and North Western Railway adopted the Underground's four rail d.c. system wholesale – there was considerable overlap with previously electrified lines and, uniquely, through running of tube trains was projected. The core of the scheme was what became known as the New Line. This was envisaged as an entirely separate, all-electric, passengers-only line from Euston to Watford. Electrification of the Broad Street-Willesden-Richmond and Willesden-Earls Court routings was tacked on later.

Watford Joint Stock, c.1922: rocking and rolling all the way to Watford with the Underground. (Author's collection)

The New Line was tackled first. The section from Willesden to Watford opened in 1911–12 and was initially steam worked. Queens Park-Willesden followed in 1915 as electric but was served by Bakerloo trains, whose extension from Paddington was paid for the North Western. Electrification continued to Watford in 1917, the Underground again providing the main service. In 1920 work was proceeding on the final stretch to Euston. This was only partly new – the Underground and North London connections were thought to compensate for the failure to duplicate through to the terminus – and included a heavily engineered series of burrowing junctions at Camden.

The West London was the first of the converted lines. Services from Earls Court to Willesden commenced on 1 May 1914. New work was limited. The section from Uxbridge Road to Kensington was already in use by the Hammersmith and City, and the District-owned Kensington-Earls Court spur had been partially electrified for stock movements to Lillie Bridge depot. Initially District trains and power were used.

The intensively used Broad Street-Richmond line was electrified on 1 October 1916. The section south of Gunnersbury had already been electrified by the District. Included was the Acton-Kew Bridge side line. On 16 April 1917 some Broad Street services were extended to Watford Junction using the New Line.

The LNWR had some lovely new trains built. Elegant and smooth running, these included generous provision for first class. The original lot of four three-car sets were placed on the West London line in late 1914. A larger batch of thirty-eight three-car sets was delivered in 1915–16 for use on the North London line. Mention must be made of the seventy-two cars of 1920 Joint Stock. Although only used on Underground services to Elephant and Castle, two-thirds were actually owned by the LNWR. Livery was chocolate and white. The power station at Stonebridge Park, rated at 20,000kW, came into use in early 1916. Here also were sheds and repair facilities.

Stonebridge Park power station, *c.*1915: the twin chimneyed monster nears completion during the Great War. (Author's collection)

Completion of the scheme came on 10 July 1922. First to go was the joint stock, withdrawn by 1931. Nine cars remained in use on the Rickmansworth and Croxley Green branches until 1939. Next off was the 1914 stock, which remained in use on the West London line until 1940. The cars were sent for a holiday at Morecambe in the early 1950s, where they remained until the mid-1960s. The later LNWR stock was withdrawn by 1960. A car of this type is on display at York's National Railway Museum. The Earls Court and Kew Bridge branches were closed in 1940 due to war damage and the North London line was rerouted to North Woolwich in the 1980s. This, however, was on a different system – the old North Western electrics had been changed to third rail outside the London Transport zone in the 1970s. Stonebridge Park was already gone, decommissioned on 30 July 1967. The New Line remains as a noble monument to the age of electric.

London and South Western

The LSWR had an intensively worked suburban network and electrification seemed an obvious step. The system chosen was roughly compatible with that of the District, since the latter used LSWR track in the Wimbledon area.

The LSWR went electric in stages: Waterloo to Wimbledon via East Putney on 25 October 1915; Putney to Clapham via Twickenham and Kingston, with the Shepperton branch, on 30 January 1916; the Hounslow Loop on 12 March

LSWR electric trains at Waterloo, c.1920: early electrics lined up and ready to go in an unusually empty station. (Author's collection)

1916; Hampton Court services on 18 June 1916; finally reaching Claygate on 20 November 1916, before the First World War stopped play.

No new stock was built. Eighty-four compartment carriages, some up to twenty years old, were reconditioned and motorised at the company's Eastleigh works. Blunt ended with prominent headcode displays, which ran in three-car sets, doubled-up during the peak. Livery is believed to have been green all over. Power was supplied from the newly built station at Durnsford Road, Wimbledon. No major alteration was required to the fabric of the lines, although the new Waterloo was in the making.

The original electric stock, subsequently labelled 3SUB, was again reconditioned in the 1940s, remaining in use for another thirty years or so. Durnsford Road went offline in 1965. Subsequently, the LSWR system spread to the whole of the southern suburbs and beyond, although the voltage was later upped to 750v. The system and trains set the standard for the south – sadly.

Annexe: Electric dreams

Outside London, electrification in Britain by 1920 was mostly found in the big northern cities. The Lancashire and Yorkshire Railway was the pioneer, converting 33 miles of its suburban lines around Liverpool and a further 13 miles in Manchester. The Liverpool electrics have been combined with the Mersey Railway, also an early electric, as the core of Merseyrail. In Manchester the line forms part of the Metrolink. Newcastle also had an extensive electric network (30 miles), now converted to overhead as part of the Tyne and Wear Metro. The Tyneside electrics were carried out by the North Eastern Railway, which converted its Shildon-Newport section in 1915 as a feasibility study in regard to electrifying its main line.

In continental Europe, electric had been mostly applied to industrial and mountain lines by 1920. Electric trains had first been successfully demonstrated in Germany. However, only Hamburg had an electric suburban railway (17 miles), the precursor of its S-Bahn. Paris was a special case. With the extension of the railways to the centre of the city at the turn of the century, two companies adopted electric working over the inner part of their routes. The Orsay station of the Paris-Orleans Railway was the first main-line electric terminus in the world and by 1920 around 16 miles of its approaches had been converted. Across the city, the Western Railway electrified some 11 miles of its new suburban route out of Invalides. An interesting project was the Athens and Piraeus Railway (16 miles), an early underground, whose country terminus closely resembled the Circle stations of London. Interestingly the original wood-panelled electric stock of 1904 remained in use on the line until 1985.

After the Richmond tramway electrification of 1888, the United States was the acknowledged master of all things electric. The first heavy conversion was carried out in Baltimore as early as 1895 and by 1920 there were hundreds of miles of electrified mountain lines, as well as vast suburban networks. New York had the largest. Out of Pennsylvania station ran lines west, to the famous Manhattan Transfer (9 miles) for long-distance traffic; and east, to the Long Island Railroad (80 miles) – the world's greatest suburban electric. The New Haven, which carried out the first long-distance electrification (72 miles, 33 in the suburban zone), and the New York Central (52 miles), operated out of Grand Central. Pennsylvania and Grand Central were converted for operational reasons, but also due to legislation – local authorities were justifiably worried about the accidents in tunnel lines. Electric working also meant that tracks could be buried underground, opening up property development above. In Philadelphia, the problematic third rail line to Atlantic City (65 miles) had been superseded by the overhead network (27 miles) out of Broad Street. In the 1930s, the Pennsylvania extended the overhead to New York and Washington (the core of the current Northeast Corridor). Over these ran the GG1, most elegant of electric locomotives. Outside the north-east, the 'juicers' took the form of the Interurban. Apart from the obscure Grimsby and Immingham Tramway, the Interurban was unknown in Britain. Essentially a supertram, this was *the* American electric.

However, the US electric empires have not fared well. The once ubiquitous Interurban has vanished, leaving much of the US without effective public transport. Outside the suburban area, the main-line electrics have all but gone too. The future of the electric lay in Europe and the Far East.

1930: THE LIGHT AND THE WATER, EARTH AND MEN

London's Industrial Railways

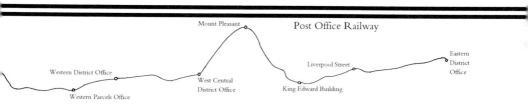

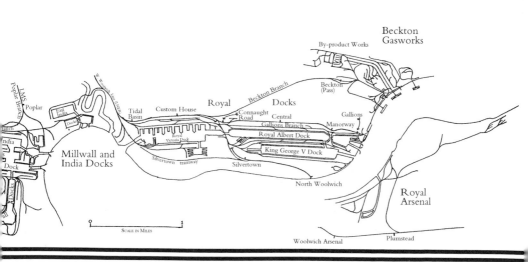

London's industrial railways in 1930.

London is not usually thought of as an industrial zone. Yet in former times, large parts of the capital were typical industrial landscapes. Much of this was a result of its size – for most of the railway century London was the biggest city in the world – and was thus a huge consumer of goods and services. This was especially true of the Port of London, the biggest port in the country, much of whose trade was in food and other necessaries. Large areas too were given over to utilities – gas and electricity production, water cleansing and sewage. All of these and more were served by internal railway systems (county of London only):

London's Industrial Railways, 1930

Industry, etc.	Location	Owner	Locos
Post Office	Whitechapel-Paddington line	General Post Office	85
Gas	Poplar gas works	Commercial Gas Co.	5
	Stepney gas works	Commercial Gas Co.	2
	Fulham gas works	Gas, Light & Coke Co.	2
	Kensal Green gas works	Gas, Light & Coke Co.	6
	Bridgefoot gas works	South Metropolitan Gas Co.	2
	East Greenwich gas works	South Metropolitan Gas Co.	23
	Old Kent Road gas works	South Metropolitan Gas Co.	2
	Ordnance Wharf tar works	South Metropolitan Gas Co.	1
	Lower Sydenham gas works	South Suburban Gas Co.	3
Docks	India and Millwall Docks	Port of London Authority	7
Military	Victualling Yard, Deptford	Admiralty	3
	Kidbrooke depot	Air Ministry	8?
	Deptford supply depot	Royal Army Service Corps	8
	Woolwich	Royal Arsenal	31?
Electricity	Grove Road power station	Central Electric Supply Co. Ltd	2
Miscellaneous	Deptford Wharf	Calders Ltd	1
	Plumstead rubbish shoot	W.R. Cunis Ltd	2
	Angerstein Wharf, Charlton	Flower & Everett Ltd	1?
	Greenwich metal works	G.A. Harvey & Co. Ltd	1
	Charlton tram depot	London County Council	1
	Battersea waterworks	Metropolitan Water Board	1?
	Woolwich works	Siemens Bros & Co. Ltd	3
	Charlton works	United Glass Bottle Mfrs Ltd	2

The industrial railways were some of the least known in the capital. Yet hidden away from public view, the little engines scuttled around, day and night, providing for London's needs. There were two basic types of industrial railway: standard gauge and narrow gauge. The former could be of great size. The latter were often self-contained systems. Motive power was usually provided by small profile

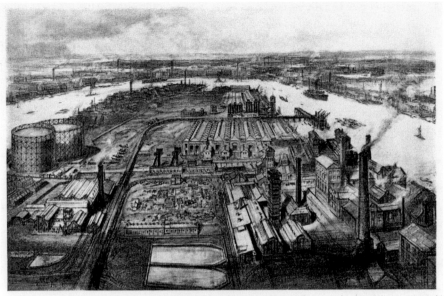

EAST GREENWICH WORKS (General View)

Greenwich gasworks, c.1930: vast swathes of London were once industrial zones – this area now houses the Millennium Dome. (From a contemporary publication)

four-coupled tank engines. It was not until 1930 or so that the number and sophistication of industrial railways reached their height. This was the heyday of such systems, which lasted until around 1960. The decline was rapid thereafter with most closed by 1970.

The Beckton Gasworks Railways

The Beckton gasworks railway impressed by its sheer size. The premises of the Gas, Light and Coke Company at Beckton were reputedly the biggest gasworks in the world. Correspondingly the site had one of London's biggest industrial railways.

The gasworks at Beckton had opened as long ago as 1870 and by 1930 occupied a huge site in East London, north of the Royal Docks. In those days, gas for domestic and commercial use was produced by heating coal at high temperatures. The process, which was carried out in 'retorts', was a very productive one as it also turned the coal into smokeless coke and gave forth useful tar and other potentially useful by-products.

A standard-gauge internal railway was provided from the very start of operations and, by 1930, was divided into three parts. The most important was that of the gasworks proper. This had both high- and low-level lines. The 9 miles of high-level track were carried on iron girders supported by concrete-filled cast iron columns, at an average of 22ft up in the air. The high-level system essentially ran from two piers at the riverside to the retort houses, and was for delivering coal for conversion or stockpiling. The low-level lines, with some 32 track miles, were primarily used for moving coke and by-products around the site. In addition, the by-products works, dealing primarily with tar, also had an internal railway. The third element was the 2 mile-long link to the North Woolwich branch at Custom House. This had a passenger service to and from Stratford operated by the London and North Eastern Railway and was also used by outgoing coke trains.

The system had around fifty locomotives, housed in three sheds, and a fully fitted works for repairs and maintenance. 0-4-0 tank engines were used exclusively. These were constructed with a short wheelbase to cope with the sharp curves in the works. The main type used were saddle tanks that were known as 'Jumbos' – possibly in a jocular fashion because of their extremely small loading gauge. Engines in use at the main gasworks site were painted apple green and the fifteen or so in the by-products works appeared in maroon.

Unlike most industrial lines the Beckton railway was run in a very professional way. It was all fully signalled and by 1930 the most part of the high level had electro-mechanical point operation, colour light signalling and track circuiting. The high level had been recently upgraded and the piers re-equipped with modern electric cranes and conveyors with delivery of coal on the high level – sped up by an automatic loading and unloading system.

Beckton gasworks locomotive, c.1930: this was No.1 of the by-products works (1892–1968), cut down for low clearances. In the background are the passenger vehicles. (Author's collection)

Beckton station, c.1930: an innumerable host waits expectantly in the picturesque east. (Unknown source)

Subsequently the gasworks went into severe decline. The passenger service from Custom House ceased in 1940 due to bombing, though it had been little patronised for some years previously. Although dieselised in 1958–9, the introduction of cheap natural gas meant the works was gradually run down in the 1960s, with production ceasing in 1969. The internal railway was abandoned the following year. Three engines formerly used at Beckton have been preserved (including examples at Bressingham and Penrhyn Castle), very little else, however, remains. A memento of the site remains as the Beckton Alps, a huge waste heap, said to be the largest artificial hill in London.

The Port of London Railways

The Port of London Authority (PLA) was the public body responsible for London's docks and navigation on the Thames. London had four dock systems (excluding the Tilbury Docks in Essex). Two of these – the Royal Docks, and the Millwall and India Docks – had internal railways. Although geographically separate, the PLA lines effectively formed a single standard-gauge railway and it was no rarity for the little blue engines to move from one waterside location to another. Unlike the Beckton system, operation was fairly primitive with, for example, little proper signalling.

PLA locomotive, 1953: potbellied no. 54 was used on the West India and Millwall Docks railways from 1915–61. (Author's collection)

PLA boat train, c.1930: the Port of London Authority had its own trains – this is a Tilbury boat train. (Author's collection)

India and Millwall Docks: This system consisted of the connected West India and Millwall Docks and the more remote East India Docks. The East India Docks were quite small and until the First World War had only a few sidings worked by horse or capstan. By 1930, there was around 2 miles of quayside track, justifying the allocation of an engine. The larger West India Docks, dealing especially with timber, had a more extensive railway system of around 7 miles, partly dating back to the 1860s, but was also worked by a single engine. The bulk of the activity was concentrated on the Millwall Docks (around 8 track miles). These dealt especially with grain and possessed a huge ten-storey granary. Millwall Docks had had an internal railway from its opening in 1868, and in 1930 was worked by seven four-coupled tank engines (six-coupled being barred because of tight curves). The Millwall and West India Docks had been recently extensively altered, removing most traces of the old passenger line in the dock area. This service, from Millwall Junction to North Greenwich, was worked by the PLA in conjunction with the Great Eastern Railway, and had been withdrawn in 1926. The Millwall-India system had connections with the Blackwall line of the LNER and the LMS's North London line.

The Royal Docks: The Royal Docks (Victoria, Albert and King George V) sprawled across a vast tract of East London and possessed an internal railway system of some 70 miles. This had begun in 1855 as a simple horse-drawn tramway at the newly opened Victoria Dock. Locomotive operation commenced in 1880 and by 1930 around twenty engines were on site. These were mainly Hudswell-Clarke six-coupled tanks, housed in a shed at Custom House. Traffic at the Royals was varied but specialities included meat and grain. The Royals had numerous clients within its bounds, including several main-line goods depots, Cory Brothers' coal jetty at Gallions, and four massive flour mills. Goods wagons to outside destinations were exchanged with main-line companies at exchange sidings near Custom House station, which ran onto the North Woolwich line at Thames Wharf. There was also a passenger line, originally the Albert Dock Railway, running from Custom House to Gallions. This was owned by the PLA but services were provided by the LNER. This was already in decline in 1930 and would be closed ten years later.

The Silvertown tramway: Mention must also be made of the Silvertown tramway. This was formerly a stretch of the North Woolwich line which passed to dock control in 1855. It was owned by the PLA but worked by the LNER and hosted a large number of riverside factories and wharves.

The PLA railways were dieselised in 1961 and closed in 1970. The last traffic on the Silvertown tramway, however, was as recently as 1991.

The Post Office Railway

The Post Office Railway (POR) was one of the least known but most interesting of London's railways. As a railway uniquely devoted to letters and parcels, this all-electric railway was a technological masterpiece of its age.

The POR was born just before the First World War. Despite the advent of electric trams and tube railways, London's main transport problem was still traffic congestion caused by horse-drawn vehicles. This was particularly irksome to the Post Office, which was required to maintain a fast and regular service. Inspired by the crop of tube railways, the Post Office decided to go underground.

A previous effort along similar lines in mid-Victorian times, the Pneumatic Despatch Railway, had not been successful. This worked on a similar system to the London and Croydon but here the whole vehicle was placed in a much larger tube. Two trial lines were built – from Euston to a nearby sorting office and from Euston to Post Office headquarters in St Martins le Grand. The scheme was not adopted, mainly due to the fact that little time was saved, and was it closed down in 1874.

The purpose of the POR was to carry received parcels and letters to main-line stations for transfer to trains elsewhere. Thus, the approximately 6½ mile-long line ran from the huge Mount Pleasant complex via a string of sorting offices to Paddington and Liverpool Street stations. Tunnels were built from 1914 to 1917, but work was then suspended due to the war, restarting in 1924. The line was finally opened in stages between December 1927 and February 1928.

Physically the POR was similar to contemporary tube railways, with tunnels of cast-iron segments, running an average of 70ft under the earth. Here however, two tracks ran through a single tunnel and the stations were equipped with passing loops. A switch man in a cabin between the platforms controlled traffic – there were no drivers, everything was under remote control. The dark-green cars were of 2ft gauge, and on to which were wheeled mail containers. A three-rail system was used with a central power rail delivering electricity rated at 440v (tunnels) and 150v (stations and sidings) direct current, which was received from outside suppliers. Chutes, conveyors and lifts took the mail to and from the surface.

THE PNEUMATIC DESPATCH TUBE : THE END OF THE TUBE AT HOLBORN ON THE OPENING DAY.—SEE PAGE 496.

Pneumatic Despatch Railway, 7 November 1865: this was the first Post Office Railway. Bearded gents were not the common cargo. (*Illustrated London News*)

In 1930 the line was still experiencing teething troubles, which centred on its ninety-strong fleet of cars. The long wheelbase of these rigid four wheelers was causing heavy track damage. The debris from this went on to cause short circuits in the cars and electrical equipment. To overcome this, the line was re-equipped with articulated stock. The old stock was withdrawn by the middle of 1931.

The year 1962 was the peak year for the POR. Latterly, the line, re-branded as Mail Rail, did not fare well. The cessation of transport of post via the railways and the decline of real mail in favour of its e-mail cousins affected it badly. The final straw was the introduction of the congestion charge. The end came on 30 May 2003, by which time the service had been cut back to Mount Pleasant-Paddington. The demise of the Post Office Railway is especially ironic considering its impeccable green credentials – the line has been moth-balled and, perhaps, will be revived by a more far-sighted regime.

The Royal Arsenal Railway

The Royal Arsenal Railway (RAR) was a government-owned ammunitions and weapons factory set on a huge site in Woolwich. In peacetime 1930, the RAR was much reduced from its height during the First World War, when no fewer than 118 engines (some on loan) were in use on a network of 120 track miles, but the Arsenal still possessed what was probably the biggest internal railway in London. Lines snaked round and into dozens of workshops and full-scale factories, as well as onto the several piers and wharves on the riverside frontage of some 4 miles. Two different gauges were used, 18in narrow gauge as well as standard gauge, with mixed-gauge tracks being commonplace. As with the PLA railways, operation was quite unsophisticated with semaphore signalling a rarity.

Narrow gauge: The narrow gauge system was based on that used at the LNWR's Crewe Works. The first locomotive was delivered in 1871 with regular working probably beginning two years later. The narrow gauge extended for a maximum of 60 miles during the First World War but was severely cut back in 1923 in favour of the standard gauge. The narrow gauge was mostly used where rail access inside buildings was required. Very sharp curves precluded use of any but four-coupled engines. Oil-fired, paraffin and diesel engines had been in use but in 1930 only four conventional steam locomotives remained. These were 'Charlton'-class 0-4-0 tanks, built by Avonside in 1915–16, provided with wide American-style spark arresters to guard against the risk of fire, and named after British cities and towns. A passenger service for workers was operated over the narrow gauge by the turn of the century. During the First World War, this provided three classes with enclosed carriages for officers and 'toast racks' for the men. This was still running in 1930 but only offered standard third accommodation.

Woolwich Arsenal Railway, c.1915: the narrow-gauge passenger service pictured at its height. (Author's collection)

Standard gauge: A primitive tramway had been authorised as early as 1824. This was entirely worked by horses until the acquisition of standard-gauge engines in 1875. By the late 1860s, the standard-gauge network was connected with the South Eastern Railway's North Kent line east of Plumstead station, through the 'Hole in the Wall'. The standard gauge was used for material being shipped out and for internal movement of larger items such as heavy guns. The standard-gauge network reached a maximum of 120 miles and in 1930 was probably not much less than that. Included were lines out into Plumstead Marshes, where the explosives and timber yards had been isolated. As with the narrow-gauge lines, four-coupled engines were used almost exclusively. These were of various manufacturers and, like their narrow-gauge counterparts, were mostly of Great War vintage. In 1930 around twenty of these were still in use. These had stirring names, including *Invincible*, *Lion* and *Liberty*, as well as the classically referenced *Arethusa*, the satanic *Lucifer* and the merely odd *Lurcher* (one hopes it didn't). Such a cache of names was quite typical of industrial railways.

Both systems endured until the end of production at the Arsenal in 1967 but were little used after the mid-1950s. *Invincible*, a standard-gauge engine, is preserved on the Isle of Wight. The largest collection of RAR artefacts, including *Woolwich*, the last working 18in-gauge locomotive in Britain and decked out in the original maroon and black livery, is at the Royal Gunpowder Mills, Waltham Abbey. On site is a section of mixed-gauge track and a gunpowder van.

Annexe: Work, Rest and Play

The Royal Arsenal was essentially a factory and its railway was a glorified conveyor belt. Berlin, on the other hand, had a proper military railway: the Royal Prussian Military Railway (Königlich Preußische Militäreisenbahn), built and operated by the army from 1875 to 1918. Starting from Schöneberg, the line ran parallel to the Dresden main line as far as Zossen, then cut across country to the small town of Jüterbog, some 70km in total. Here, specialist troops gained practical experience in railway operations, transporting soldiers and heavy weapons to the artillery range at Kummersdorf, as well as running regular passenger and goods services, with their fleet of eighteen locomotives. The main line to Zossen was closed after the transfer to the civic authorities, while the continuation to Jüterbog remained in branch use until the 1990s. The latter section is now in use as a *Draisinenbahn*, a German rail speciality on which leisure trips can be taken on manually powered trolleys.

Fortuitously, London had no need for a ship canal – the river was quite adequate. However, such channels brought forth interesting railways. Most fascinating are those of the Panama Canal. At Gatun, Pedro Miguel and Miraflores, 5ft gauge, electric locomotives guide ships through the locks, via cables attached to integral winches. The lock railways are entirely isolated and work on the rack and pinion system for maximum traction. The 'mules', as they are known, were originally US products, but since 1964 have been Mitsubishi built. There are some 108 units. Examples of the older type have been preserved at various locations along the canal and at the Virginia Museum of Transportation.

Also at Beckton was the establishment dealing with the waste products of the north side of London, again allegedly the biggest of its type in the world. The sewage works, however, did not use rail to any extent. Sewage by rail was by no means rare, with many British cities having internal systems. Less common was the sewer tourism of Paris. Here, in the wide-built tunnels whose construction commenced in 1850, visitors were treated to a combined rail and boat trip from Châtelet to the Madelaine. In 1894–5 the service was electrified, 100v, tram style. Alas, rail tours are no longer offered. A sample of the rolling stock is preserved at the Paris Sewers Museum.

Similar in intent to the Post Office Railway was the Chicago freight subway. This underground goods railway opened in 1906 and, by its peak in the late 1920s, had 59 miles of tunnel, and transported 600,000 tons per year with its 149 locomotives. The freight subway was not a technological innovation: it used conventional mining locomotives, fitted with manual braking, and minimal signalling. For power, 2ft-gauge overhead trolley wires were used. The titchy tunnels, 6ft 7in wide by 7ft 6in high, and lined with concrete, were carved by hand through the blue clay 40ft below downtown. Private sidings into the basements of railroad depots, shops, offices and factories were augmented by public stations.

Paris sewers railway, 1870: top hats and crinolines enjoy the ride on the poopy express. (*Illustrated London News*)

Chicago freight subway: a really good idea which never really took off. (Author's collection)

Connection to the surface was by lifts, conveyors and inclines. Traffic was general goods, coal, ashes and rubbish, and, briefly (1906–8), post. The subway closed in 1959, mainly due to road competition: trucks had greater capacity, could easily transport oversize items, and provided direct service without transhipment. After closure, the locos were sold for scrap, except for two left stranded. The last loads of ash were also left where they stood. The tunnels are still there today, some reused as conduits for pipes and cables.

The City's Railways Blitzed

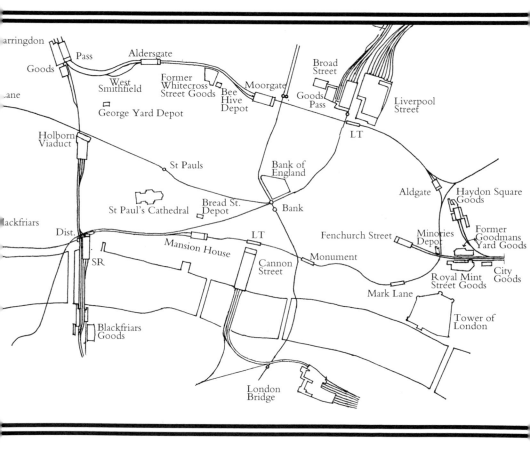

Railways in the City of London, 1940.

In 1940 the City of London would be both familiar and unfamiliar to the modern city worker. As with now, banking and finance were the most prominent industries of the ancient square mile. The Bank of England sat like a spider in the middle of a web of narrow streets, dotted with tiny ancient churches and queer little halls: relics of medieval times. Clustered around were the head offices of the big national and international banks, insurance firms and so forth. Close by was the Stock Exchange, smaller and more exclusive than at present. Important also were the other exchanges – Corn and Baltic included. Offices dominated the scene. However, the majority were petty affairs, as portrayed in J.B. Priestley's *Angel Pavement*. These paper mills were fed by vast battalions of commuters disgorged from the major stations:

Main Line Stations in the City of London, 1940

Blackfriars	Southern Railway
Broad Street	LMS and LNER trains
Cannon Street	Southern Railway
Fenchurch Street	LNER and LMS trains
Holborn Viaduct	Southern Railway
Liverpool Street	LNER
London Bridge	Southern Railway

Both the LNER and the LMS also ran trains to Moorgate via the City Widened Lines and the Great Western Railway ran commuter trains to Aldgate on the Metropolitan.

Further flows emerged from the subterranean world of the London Passenger Transport Board (LPTB). The lines of the LPTB, commonly known as London Transport, were divided between the subsurface lines of the District and Metropolitan and the deep-level tubes. Two of the latter served the City, the Northern and the Central Lines, crossing at Bank – the biggest station on the system. There was also the Northern City, formerly the Great Northern and City Railway and later part of the Great Northern Electrics, but then a self-contained portion (Finsbury Park–Moorgate) of the Northern Line. Hammersmith and City, and Circle services also served the City but were then regarded as part and parcel of the Metropolitan Line.

Underground Stations in the City of London, 1940

Aldersgate and Barbican	Metropolitan Line
Aldgate	Metropolitan Line
Bank	Central and Northern lines, Waterloo and City
Blackfriars	District Line

Cannon Street	District Line
Chancery Lane	Central Line
Farringdon	Metropolitan Line
Liverpool Street	Central and Metropolitan Lines
London Bridge	Northern Line
Mansion House	District Line
Mark Lane	District Line
Monument	District Line
Moorgate	Metropolitan, Northern and Northern City Lines
St Pauls	Central Line

There also existed the Waterloo and City Railway, a shuttle line owned and operated by the Southern Railway and terminating at Bank.

The City, however, was far from being the money-grabbing monoculture of today. Then, the area was an important warehousing district, particularly of textiles, and was home to two big wholesale markets, Smithfield for meat and Billingsgate for fish (the latter now decamped tothe East End, the former a shadow of its old self). To serve the productive elements of the economy the City was provided with a range of goods depots:

Goods Depots in the City of London, 1940

Blackfriars	Southern Railway
Broad Street	London, Midland and Scottish Railway
City Goods	London, Midland and Scottish Railway
Farringdon Street	London and North Eastern Railway
Haydon Square	London, Midland and Scottish Railway
Royal Mint Street	London and North Eastern Railway
Smithfield	Great Western Railway

A further depot, Whitecross Street, had closed down four years previously, and another, Goodmans Yard, had been absorbed into Royal Mint Street. Also worthy of mention is tiny, all-electric Vine Street, the Metropolitan's City Goods station, again closed in 1936. Farringdon Street and the wholly underground Smithfield were situated off the City Widened Lines; Haydon Square, Royal Mint Street and City Goods were accessed by the line to Fenchurch Street; Broad Street was adjacent to the passenger station. Blackfriars was located south of the river, opposite its passenger counterpart. These ranged in size from the petty to the prestigious.

In addition the City was provided with a number of receiving offices. Although not rail-connected, these were very important parts of the goods system, functioning as forward posts, taking in small items and passing these on to the main stations, issuing tickets and giving out information. The most important offices, usually referred to as depots, and, indeed, marginally smaller than the smallest goods depots, were:

Receiving Offices in the City of London, 1940

44–47 Bread Street	London and North Eastern Railway
118 Minories	Great Western Railway
George Yard, West Smithfield	London, Midland and Scottish Railway
'Bee Hive', Whitecross Street	London and North Eastern Railway

There were others of less importance, but none were owned by the Southern. This complex and intricate transport network was about to become the front line.

The Second Great Fire of London

The times given in this section are from fire brigade records and state when the fire was first reported. Especially for the larger blazes, the time is approximate.

The period around Christmas was always quiet in the City, more so than ever this year, with many businesses having evacuated to the country. The 29 December was a Sunday night, always the lowest ebb in the city's life. The Blitz, which had started four months earlier, had hushed down. Apart from a few desultory forays, such as the one a couple of nights before, the Luftwaffe had scarcely shown its face over the capital since the end of the period of nightly raids some six weeks previously. So there were fewer shelterers in the deep tube stations in the area than had been the case during the 'Old Blitz' of September and October.

The bombers began to come over just after teatime, as had become traditional. Despite claims to the contrary, this was not a heavy raid. Surprisingly few planes were involved and many of these scattered their bombs over other parts of London. Perhaps only a few dozen dropped their loads of incendiaries in a fairly concentrated pattern over the City. Some fell on roads and burnt out. Others fell on the handful of buildings with teams of firewatchers (such as St Paul's Cathedral). These were mostly soon dealt with. A good proportion, however, fell on unoccupied buildings, which soon caught light. The danger came not from these isolated fires but from the sparks and burning debris given off. These set fire to adjacent buildings and before long, fanned by a west wind, great chunks of the City were a seething cauldron of fire. Chance hits on water mains and low tide meant there was little chance of meaningful action.

6.15p.m. Aldersgate and Moorgate stations, former Whitecross Street goods depot

The main fire zone was located to the north of the City in a belt stretching from Aldersgate Street to Finsbury Pavement, and north from Cheapside to Old Street. Snaking its way through this district of tall warehouses was the Circle line between Aldersgate and Moorgate stations.

At Aldersgate the booking office building, a three-storey affair with quoins to the central section and dating back to the line's opening in the 1860s, was largely burnt out. Within a few weeks a temporary booking office was put up in the shell of the ground floor. The great arched roof behind had been shattered by a near miss in November. The station was redeveloped in the 1960s – Sir John Betjeman's 'Monody on the death of Aldersgate Street station' commemorates its sad fate.

The destruction at Moorgate was far worse. The platforms were swept by fire, destroying all the canopies and other structures and damaging beyond repair the old electric locomotive of the City and South London Railway positioned incongruously on the concourse. Damage was also sustained by an electric train stranding at the station. The towering block of late Victorian offices, which formed the street frontage, also went west. From here the blaze crept over to the

Moorgate station, c.1905: in the towering metropolis before the war. (Author's collection)

Moorgate station, c.1945: the ruins after the Blitz. (Author's collection)

Northern line building between Moorfields and Finsbury Pavement. This was formerly the head offices of the City and South London Railway. Part of the roof and top storey was burnt out, but luckily the fire was brought under control before further damage was done (the missing part was later restored and it is now difficult to believe that this building was damaged at all).

Between the two was the former goods depot at Whitecross Street, disused but intact. This had been opened by the Midland Railway in 1878. The huge red-brick warehouse that formed the frontage burned down. The rear portion survived with only minor damage and was used as a handy escape route down to the tracks for firemen and shelterers cut off in the centre of the blaze. After the war this area was a vast empty no-man's-land in the middle of the capital.

6.35p.m. St Paul's Underground station

There were several minor fire areas. That around St Paul's Cathedral developed at the same time as the Cripplegate fire. This centred on the publishing district, which, chock full of paper, was a disaster waiting to happen. Paternoster Square was reduced to a shambles of burnt-out buildings. The underground station serving this area was badly hit. The old exit building on the corner of King Edward Street, a typical Central London Railway building of 1900 with terracotta tile facing and red-brick upper storeys, was gutted. The ruins were demolished some years after the war. The newer exit, dating from the interwar period, was set in a building opposite St Martin's le Grand. Here the upper storeys were burnt away but the exit itself remained usable.

Whitecross Street, c.1899: the huge ornate warehouse is to the right. (From a contemporary publication)

Whitecross Street, c.1945: this whole district was rendered a wasteland. (Author's collection)

6.51p.m. Royal Mint Street goods station

Slightly later another big blaze developed around the Minories. This area had been previously damaged during the first raids in early September, when the Haydon Square depot had been all but destroyed. The LNER goods depot in this area, Royal Mint Street, had also been previously damaged. This raid completed

Post Office station, *c*.1905: spic and span not long after opening. (Author's collection)

St Paul's station area, *c*.1945: the bombed out ruin, to the right is the old station building. (Author's collection)

the work. The northern section, originally the Great Eastern's Goodmans Yard depot was totally destroyed and the eastern half of the former Great Northern premises to the south, dating from the turn of the century, largely gutted. Twenty-nine wagons were destroyed here.

7p.m. Blackfriars goods station

One of the few high explosives to fall in the central area on that night fell on the warehouse of Blackfriars goods station. This crumbled a wall but made little real difference as the building had been burnt out six weeks earlier.

7p.m. Holborn Viaduct station

There were a large number of smaller fires that night which were easily got under control. At Holborn Viaduct damage was limited to the destruction of the 'Shunters Lobby' (presumably some form of hut) on platform six.

Holborn Viaduct station, 1874: here is the grandiose frontage towering up with row upon row of windows. (*The Builder*)

Holborn Viaduct station, *c.*1955: there is nothing left but a fragment of the ground floor. (Photograph from unknown source)

7.07p.m. Blackfriars station

More serious was the fire that burned down the upper half of the Blackfriars District line station. This was a splendid building in the Moorish style, designed by one F.J. Ward, with ornate balconies and topped by squat little minarets. The lower two floors lasted into the 1980s as a sad ruin.

7.30p.m. London Bridge station

To the City worker the next morning the most noticeable damage was to London Bridge station – the doyen of the City stations. The station had received its due allotment of incendiaries at around 6.30p.m. but these had been quickly extinguished. Around an hour later, burning debris from nearby fires came to rest on the roof of the parcels office. The fire spread quickly and the Central Section (former LBSCR station) and the General Offices (the former hotel) were set alight. The station was evacuated at 8p.m. The old hotel was completely destroyed and the upper floors of the Central section were burnt out. The South Eastern half of the station was similarly dealt with the following April. The ruins lasted into the 1970s.

7.40p.m. Fenchurch Street station

Probably as a result of the overspill of the Minories fire there was some fire damage to Fenchurch Street station and the signal box rendered out of use.

7.45p.m. Bread Street receiving office

The LNER receiving office at 44-47 Bread Street was also destroyed during the raid. Opened in May 1887 by the Great Northern Railway, it was one of the City's largest and most important. The LNER also lost its Beehive depot in Whitecross Street, opposite the old Midland goods depot, on this night.

Perhaps overall the City's transport infrastructure escaped lightly. Delays were caused mainly by unsafe buildings overhanging the line rather than destruction of railway structures. The tube, with its cache of shelterers, was scarcely affected.

London Bridge station, c.1930: as a German bomber pilot might have seen it. (Author's collection)

Elsewhere on this night, Waterloo was affected by fire to platforms 7 and 8. Worse damage was caused when an anti-aircraft shell fell within one of the underground arches, shredding signalling cables that were vital to the efficient running of the system. Most of the delays could be traced to this own goal, rather than the raid itself. Bricklayers Arms goods was also damaged on this night – seventy-two items of rolling stock were damaged in and around K Shed.

After the Second Great Fire

The Blitz was far from over. Two weeks later, on the night of 11 January, came the terrible disaster at Bank: 112 dead when the roof of the booking office caved in after a direct hit. This was a truly horrendous event, with the blast travelling down passageways and blowing passengers onto the track. The casualty figure was elevated due to the fact that shelterers had to come to the surface to use the toilets. Even such deep dugouts were no proof against direct hits. Further bombs hit a subway at St Paul's tube and bit chunks out of Liverpool Street main line station. The spring saw the Blitz heat up again. The City largely escaped damage during the large-scale raids in March and April, although Farringdon Street goods depot was mostly destroyed during the massive raid of 'The Wednesday' (16 April).

The worst came at the very end of the Blitz: the terrible night of 10 May 1941. All the main-line stations in the City were damaged. At Liverpool Street the roof of the west side office building was set alight and the upper floors were

City of London, c.1945: from this high up the City looks undamaged. (Author's collection)

badly damaged. The old London and Blackwall offices at Fenchurch Street were destroyed and the whole station was badly blasted. Down at Cannon Street the old hotel was ablaze and the train shed mangled. Holborn Viaduct also took a packet and the hotel frontage burnt down.

After the Blitz the City was a sorry sight but, like the rest of London, it carried on.

Annexe: Rivers of Babylon

Bombed and burnt, London's stations carried on as part of the life of the capital. In continental Europe on the other hand, railway stations were becoming places of death. Today, 'death stations' dot the map from the Atlantic to the Urals.

In 1940, Berlin was the 'heart of darkness'. Here, the deportations had already begun. The procedure was to become familiar. First, receipt of the *Evakuierungsbefehl* (evacuation order). Next, assembly at a central hall or similar. Finally, next morning, the march to the station, where *Sonderzüge* (special trains) awaited them.

From ordinary stations, *Altertransporte* (trains of regular passenger stock) departed to Theresienstadt, the 'model camp' (really a squalid waiting room for the gas chambers) that was reserved for Great War veterans, etc: 123 such trains left Berlin. Of the 15,000 thus transported, 9,600 passed through the Anhalter station – a plaque now commemorates them.

Anhalter station, Berlin, c.1905: first an elegant piece of transport Victoriana, later a monster in the heart of darkness, now a forgotten relic. (Author's collection)

The *Osttransporte*, consisting of cattle trucks, were sent to the Polish Ghettos and later directly to Sobibor and Auschwitz. In some sixty-one transports, 35,000 Berliners met this fate. Seventeen (late 1941 to July 1942) departed from Grunewald – a quiet stop on the S-Bahn to Wetzlar. Here is the main memorial to those deported from Berlin, known as Gleis 17, from the track in the goods yard used. Later (August 1942 to April 1943), twenty transports departed from Moabit goods station on the Ringbahn. There is a plaque on the bridge by Putlitzer Strasse. The starting point of twenty-four later transports is not recorded but was probably also Moabit.

The Jews of France were gathered at Drancy, a modern housing estate on the outskirts of Paris. Beginning in early 1942, around 65,000 people were sent east, mainly to their deaths at Auschwitz. Drancy-le-Bourget station on the Grande Ceinture, was originally used. The departure point was soon switched to nearby Bobigny, a closed station in use only for goods. Twenty-one transports (22,400 people) left here from 18 July 1943 to 31 July 1944. The station is currently being converted to a memorial.

At Budapest's Jozsefvaros station, formerly the North station and recently closed, a plaque commemorates Raoul Wallenberg, to whom the last functional Jewish community in Eastern Europe owes much. In the summer of 1944 the Germans began the clearance of the city's Jews. By distributing 'passports', Wallenberg saved perhaps 50,000 Jews. The same number, however, were sent to their deaths in Auschwitz from this station. Wallenberg died ignominiously in Soviet custody.

The largest deportation occurred at the *Umschlagplatz* (trans-shipment point) of the Warsaw Ghetto. During the *Grossaktion Warsaw* from 22 July to 12 September 1942, some 265,000 were sent to their deaths at Treblinka. The *Umschlagplatz* (the name was also used at other camps) was a walled off section of the Gdansk goods station accessed by a branch off Warsaw's ring railway. The recently erected memorial represents a goods truck, its doors standing wide to receive the condemned.

The familiar face of the local railway station was the last the deported saw of the ordinary world. The station memorials are a permanent reminder of the role of the railways in the slaughter of the Holocaust: *Niemals Vergessen*.

1950: BASE DETAILS

London's Engine Sheds

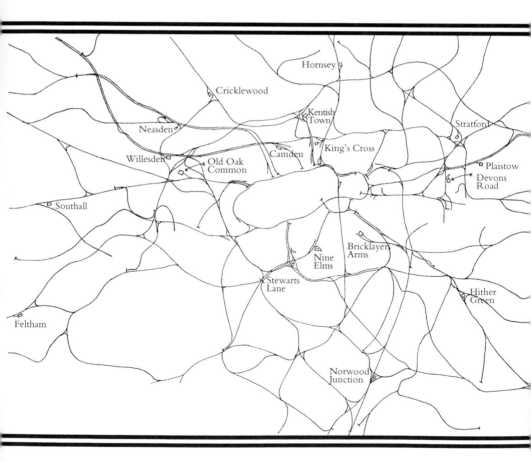

London's engine sheds in 1950.

The year 1950 was a good year for visiting the sheds. Not only was it was relatively easy for rail fans to gain access, but the range of engines was at its height. Pre-grouping stock still lingered, giving a flavour of nostalgia, but the flamboyant new locomotives of the 1930s, especially the distinctive Pacific (4-6-2) classes, some streamlined, were more exciting. Those sheds stabling such big beasts, for example Top Shed at King's Cross, were the enthusiast's favourite, however, there were many others of less fame but equal importance for the spotter to enjoy.

Engine Sheds in London, 1950

British Railways region	Shed code*	Name	Total engines
London Midland Region	1A	Willesden	135
	1B	Camden	56
	1D	Devons Road	48
	14A	Cricklewood	89
	14B	Kentish Town	117
Eastern Region	30A	Stratford	383
	33A	Plaistow	83
	34A	King's Cross	160
	34B	Hornsey	81
	34E	Neasden	82
Southern Region	70A	Nine Elms	99
	70B	Feltham	77
	73A	Stewarts Lane	112
	73B	Bricklayers Arms	140
	73C	Hither Green	51
	75C	Norwood Junction	38
Western Region	81A	Old Oak Common	193
	81C	Southall	71

* *Shed codes: British Railways adopted the London, Midland and Scottish Railway system in 1948, extending it to other regions by 1950.*

So far as the companies north of the river were concerned, little had changed since late Victorian times. The northern and western sheds were organised in pairs, one for goods and local passenger locos, and one for express machines. Thus, ex-Great Western Old Oak Common housed mostly express passenger engines, with Southall primarily for goods work. The other pairs were: Camden and Willesden (ex-LNWR); Kentish Town and Cricklewood (once Midland); King's Cross and Hornsey (ex-GNR).

To the south, big changes had occurred since Grouping, with four sheds (ratty little New Cross, neat Battersea Park, West Croydon and Slade Green) lost to steam and two replacements opened (Norwood and Hither Green).

King's Cross shed, 28 November 1954: woe betide the unauthorised spotter. (Author's collection)

London Midland Region

Willesden

Despite its prestigious code, Willesden was by no means the premier shed of London, housing locomotives for goods (such as LMS-era 8F 2-8-0s) and local passenger work (big tanks like the 3MT 2-6-2s) on what is now the West Coast main line out of Euston. But the billowing clouds of steam, the looming structures, the smell of coal smoke and the hiss of the engines were quite representative of the steam era depot. There were two actual sheds. The older, dating back to 1873 and enlarged in 1898, was of the conventional 'straight' type (rectangular in plan with external turntables). This was in bad repair, having had its roof partly demolished just before the war. Supplementing this was a modern (1929) 'square roundhouse' (with tracks radiating outwards from a central internal turntable). All buildings were demolished after closure in 1965. The site is now a goods depot dealing with containers.

Camden

Although not particularly large, Camden was a prime site for spotting main-line steam. Here could be seen the famous streamlined Coronation Pacifics ('Big Lizzies'), the most powerful steam locomotives in Britain, as well as other biggies such as the Royal Scots. The site, hemmed in by houses and equipped with miserly buildings, was unworthy of such honours. During the 1930s, the old

Willesden shed,
23 December 1962:
this pair of very
evocative images sums
up the romance of the
shed – huge clouds
of steam, towering
dark shapes, and the
round-profiled objects
of desire. (Author's
collection)

Willesden shed,
23 December 1962.
(Author's collection)

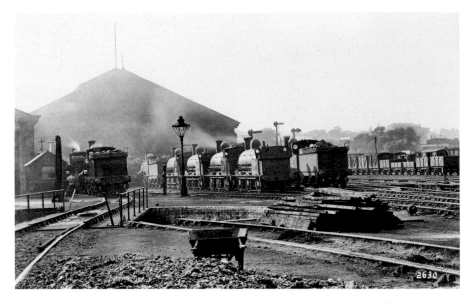

Camden shed, *c.*1900: the shed was a mucky place with unexplained piles of things lying about ready for mysterious purposes. (Author's collection)

engine shed, with its huge gabled roof dating back to 1847, had been rebuilt with a dull but functional flat roof. Across the tracks was a reminder of earlier times, a true roundhouse (rare in Britain but almost universal in the US). This had been a gin warehouse since Victorian times and survives today as a theatre. The end of steam came in 1962; diesels stayed briefly and the shed closed in 1966. Carriage sidings occupy the site.

Devons Road

With electrification of the western section of the North London line, and the closure to passengers of the eastern section, Devons Road was in severe decline. Nonetheless, it had a fair allocation of six-coupled tank engines (like 'Thomas') for goods traffic. Only one of the two original buildings of 1882, backing Limehouse Cut, still survived. The shed was in good repair, having been re-roofed in 1946. The depot had the distinction of being the first completely diesel depot after the last steamer was expelled in 1958. The shed was closed six years later. The site has been redeveloped.

Cricklewood

Like Willesden, Cricklewood (originally known as Childs Hill) was primarily for goods engines, mainly dull six-coupled types working the Midland main line out of St Pancras. However, this was the only place in London where one could regularly see Garratt articulateds, Britain's biggest locomotives, which headed

Cricklewood shed, *c.*1900: the queer-shaped constructions hanging down are smoke hoods for extracting exhaust gases. (Author's collection)

Coal hopper, Cricklewood shed, *c.*1930: once a familiar sight – coal wagons were lifted up and their vital contents deposited inside ready for fuelling up a loco. (Author's collection)

coal trains from the north terminating at the yards here. Cricklewood had two square roundhouses, dating from 1882 and 1893, both in good repair, having been re-roofed in 1949. After the end of steam at the depot in 1964, diesels were in residence for a while. The buildings were mostly demolished in 1969. Surviving on the site is the old repair shop, which had passed into commercial hands as long ago as the 1920s.

Kentish Town

Although a large depot, exciting engines were seldom seen here. Tank engines and 'second stringers', such as the 4-6-0 Jubilees, formed the bulk of the stud, which was almost exclusively passenger orientated. There were three square roundhouses, all recently re-roofed. No. 1 of 1868, 'The Metro', was used for tanks on services to Moorgate over the Metropolitan. Nos 2 and 3 dated from 1899. After closure in 1963, most of the buildings passed into private hands.

Eastern Region

Stratford

This, the largest depot in the country, served the extensive ex-Great Eastern empire. The depot had a large variety of locomotives for all types of traffic, but most numerous were the N7 0-6-2Ts for local goods work. The main building was the busy 'Jubilee Shed', dating from Queen Victoria's golden jubilee year of 1887. This had been rebuilt after war damage but was still an unpleasant and odorous place. Adjacent was the dilapidated and misleadingly named 'New Shed' of 1871, which was used for minor repairs. Overlooking the sheds was the huge but antiquated 800-ton coaling plant. A quaint vestige of the old days existed in the form of a roundhouse of 1840, then in use by Stratford Works. Stratford closed for steam in 1962, a diesel depot continued on the site until recently. Stratford City, the mixed-use development built for the 2012 Olympic Games, and the new Stratford International station, occupy the location today. Stratford's outstations included small sheds at Enfield, Epping, Spitalfields, Walthamstow (Wood Street) and Palace Gates.

Stratford works, 1938: the shed was ensconced in the works – handy for repair work. (Author's collection)

Plaistow shed, *c.*1910: this is the first shed with a selection of big tanks ready for use outside. (Author's collection)

Plaistow

Plaistow served the former LTSR lines. Tank engines, primarily for short–distance passenger work, were the main machines present. A variety of classes were in use, although 4-4-2T and 2-6-4T classes were most prominent. The building was relatively new, dating back to 1911. The roof, renewed in the 1930s, was cut back after bomb damage. The first shed, of 1899, had been taken for use by the locomotive, carriage and wagon works in Edwardian times. The works closed in LMS days, but the buildings, including the old engine shed, survive in commercial use. Plaistow closed in 1962, after electrification of the line, and the second shed was demolished.

King's Cross

Known as 'Top Shed', not for its superlative status, although that was real enough, but to distinguish it from the long departed Bottom Shed (a dark and smelly hole), King's Cross housed a range of goods and passenger engines. Most numerous were N2 0-6-2 tanks for suburban and local goods work, but there was also a stud of J52 0-6-0 saddle tanks, sturdy little goods engines. 'The Cross' was famous for its line up of big-named engines, such as the famous streamlined A4 Pacifics (like *Mallard*, the fastest steam locomotive of all) and the earlier A3 class (e.g. 4472 *Flying Scotsman*). The buildings were in excellent condition, having been re-roofed the previous year after bomb damage, and consisted of two sheds. 'The Crescent', built in 1851, was partly used for repairs, with the northern section, known as 'The Met', housing local goods and passenger engines. In front was an eight-road straight shed, partly dating back to 1862, for the bigger locomotives. The depot was closed in 1963 upon dieselisation of the main line. Its buildings were demolished the following year.

Hornsey

Opened in 1899, Hornsey housed mainly local goods and shunting engines, such as the class J52 0-6-0 saddle tanks, the archetypal residents, although some locomotives for suburban passenger work were also to be found here. The brick-built shed with

Above: King's Cross shed, c.1910: 'Top Shed' with a selection of odd structures and smart express engines. (Author's collection)

Left: Incident at Hornsey shed, January 1907: water was the other essential for the functioning of a steam locomotive. Cramped conditions could often lead to accidents. (Author's collection)

ACCIDENT AT HORNSEY STATION.—A remarkable accident happened at Hornsey Railway Station on Monday evening. In connection with the extensive locomotive sheds on the Harringay side there is a high level coal stage, and by some means a waggon of coal was pushed through the dead end. It pulled out the stays of a huge water tank built at the end of the staging. The cast-iron plates of the tank gave way, and the rush of water carried away the greater portion of one side of the tank. Fortunately no one was injured, but as a result of the accident the water supply has been cut off, and the engines cannot now be cleaned or have their water-tanks replenished at that station.

its industrial-style north light roof was in relatively good repair having been rebuilt in 1921. The depot was chiefly noted for its proximity to housing, which meant that it required close attention to smoke production. After closure in 1961 the shed was used for diesels for a decade or so and later as part of an electric suburban train depot.

Neasden

The old Great Central's London shed was opened in 1899 and had an allocation mainly of big tank engines, such as 2-6-4s, for long-distance suburban work. The shed itself was a medium-sized building with a north light roof, and was in relatively good repair. After closure in 1962, the site was redeveloped.

Southern Region

Nine Elms

This shed served the passenger needs of the former South Western main line out of Waterloo as well as goods traffic from Nine Elms. As such there was a mixed bag of engines stabled here but in 1950 express engines, such as the Merchant Navy and Battle of Britain Pacifics, were most noticeable. There were two sheds, standing side by side: the older western shed of 1885, extended in 1889 had been badly bashed in the Blitz and had had its roof cut back; and the New Shed of 1910. Unusually all movements to and from the sheds had to be made via the turntable. When it closed in 1967 this was the last steam shed in London. Its closure was certainly the end of an era. Not a sausage remains of the old sheds which have been thoroughly expunged.

Nine Elms shed, c.1905: the really big southern shed. (Author's collection)

Feltham

Brought into use in 1922, Feltham was the first modern shed, a Southern Railway role model. Built entirely of concrete, by 1950, the drawbacks of this material were beginning to be felt – the experience cannot have been pleasant. The shed, used mainly by goods engines, closed in 1967 and has been demolished.

Stewarts Lane

Stewarts Lane served a variety of functions but was noted for its big named engines, such as the West Country and Battle of Britain Pacifics, serving the Victoria expresses. Parts of the shed dated back to 1877 but it had been largely rebuilt in 1934 after the closure of nearby Battersea Park. The first shed on the site had opened in 1862 to serve the London, Chatham and Dover Railway and had originally been known as Longhedge, being renamed Battersea under the SECR regime, before becoming Stewarts Lane in 1934. After the end of steam in 1963 part of the old shed was converted to a diesel depot. There is still a residual railway presence in the area.

Bricklayers Arms

'The Brick' was not noted for its spectacular array of engines, which were mainly freight-orientated, although passenger machines for Kent Coast services also featured. The 1950 allocation gives a false impression as forty or so were old nags from New Cross on their way to the knacker's yard. The depot possessed three smallish sheds, all of which were old and in bad condition. The Old Shed of 1847, extended in the mid-1880s, had been partially re-roofed before the war. The New Shed of 1869 stood at right angles to this and had been a desolate ruin since the Blitz. St Patrick's Shed was a former carriage shed of 1844 that had been used for stabling engines since about 1900. Bricklayers Arms had been an important shed in Victorian times with a large range of passenger engines. However, the 1920s electrification had robbed it of suburban trade and the diversion of Continental services to Victoria took much of the rest. The depot closed in 1962 and has been totally wiped off the map. Stabling points attached to Bricklayers Arms were located at Ewer Street and New Cross.

Hither Green

Opened in 1933, this was a modern concrete shed with a north light pattern roof. Used for goods engines, such as the wartime-built WD 2-8-0s, working the adjacent marshalling yard, the shed saw its last steam engines in 1961 but continued in use for servicing diesels until 1985. It is now a permanent way depot.

Norwood Junction

Like Hither Green this was a new shed, only opened in 1935 and intended to replace New Cross (although the latter did not close until 1949 in the event). Freight engines, such as E4 class 0-6-2Ts were the main business. Closed in 1964 and subsequently demolished, the site is used for storing railway supplies.

Western Region

Old Oak Common

This depot chiefly provided express passenger locomotives for the ex-GWR lines out of Paddington. In 1950, the depot housed a fine array of 'Castles', 'Kings' and 'Halls' (all 4-6-0s), as well as a smaller stud of pannier tank engines (like 'Duck' the Great Western Engine) mainly for local goods work. Old Oak Common was the descendant of two previous sheds, Paddington (1838–52) and Westbourne Park (1852–1906), and opened on 17 March 1906. It took the unusual form of a group of four sheds with internal turntables, accommodating 112 locomotives. The complex, designed by G.J. Churchward, the chief locomotive superintendent of the GWR, was thoroughly up to date, and included a large lifting shop and all the relevant service buildings. Apart from the main shed, which was demolished in 1964, most of the old buildings still survive.

Southall

Southall was mostly used for goods engines working in the ex-GWR London area. These were mainly the 5700 Class 0-6-0 pannier tanks (a form of side tank, common in Belgium). The shed dated from 1884, succeeding a smaller building of 1859 serving the Brentford branch. Subsequently, it was rebuilt in modern fashion in 1953–4. After the end of steam in 1966 the depot housed and serviced DMUs until closure in 1986. The shed and its attendant buildings still stand and are used by a railway preservation group.

Annexe: The Land of Make Believe

The universal allocation of shed codes was a direct result of the nationalisation of Britain's railways on 1 January 1948. On this date, the newly formed British Transport Commission took over the Big Four (LMS, LNER, GWR and SR) and some fifty-five other companies, in addition to the LPTB, previously under local authority control. Britain's experience was unusual, in that it was thorough, including all common carrier lines, and all but unprecedented, in that central government had never before owned any part of the railway system.

The extent of British railway nationalisation can only be compared to that in the Communist east. Typical is the East German nationalisation of 1 April 1949, when some 112 concerns, all the non-state lines in the zone, were nationalised. The large number is, however, misleading. These were all small concerns, some narrow gauge or light, a good proportion local authority owned (the *Kreisbahnen*), and many of the rest in state hands due to the emigration of the owners. Most of Germany's railways were in the hands of the governments of the princely states by the 1880s, with a unified national network, the *Reichsbahn*, emerging after the end of the First World War.

Although state ownership in the homeland was frowned on, the British were keen nationalisers elsewhere. Within a decade of the opening of the first railway in India, the first line became state owned, and by 1900 the majority were too, although for a further quarter-century most remained worked by private companies. In Raj times there was a wide range of public ownership, with provinces, districts and the princely states, as well as central government, having stakes. After independence, British capital was quickly eliminated. However, a few Indian-owned companies continued, so it might be said that Indian railways have never been completely nationalised.

The most feted nationalisation was in Argentina, where, on 1 March 1948, seven massive British companies were ceremonially turned over to the left nationalist government of Juan Perón. The state was no stranger to railway ownership having been in control of lines, particularly in the less developed north of the country, since Victorian times. The act was a popular symbol of liberation from foreign control. However, it was costly. Far from helping the economic recovery of the country, as was intended, compensation was paid for by printing money, fuelling inflation. Subsequently, the railways became huge loss makers leading to privatisation in the 1990s.

Due to the timing of the main wave of nationalisation, state ownership has come to be viewed as a political act of the left. True, the immediate post-war era was full of the rhetoric of communalistic hope. Reality, however, was more prosaic. British railway nationalisation was pragmatic, bailing out a failing sector as part of a plan to boost development. Not so privatisation. Enamoured by the ideologues of the right, Britain's rulers became convinced that private was best for all things, including the railways, regardless of historical experience or international observation. The results are telling. Repeated collapses have meant that large swathes of the railway network are back in state hands. Ground ownership returned early and a number of the Train Operating Companies are owned in part or in full by foreign governments. A sensible response is that, due to the unprofitability of the sector, privatisation is expensive and unworkable. Sadly, our masters have yet to come to this (rather obvious) conclusion.

Index